Network Science with Python and NetworkX Quick Start Guide

Explore and visualize network data effectively

Edward L. Platt

BIRMINGHAM - MUMBAI

Network Science with Python and NetworkX Quick Start Guide

Commissioning Editor: Amey Varangaonkar
Acquisition Editor: Sandeep Mishra
Content Development Editor: Smit Carvalho
Technical Editor: Diksha Wakode
Copy Editor: Safis Editing
Project Coordinator: Kinjal Bari
Proofreader: Safis Editing
Indexer: Tejal Daruwale Soni
Graphics: Alishon Mendonsa
Production Coordinator: Jyoti Chauhan

First published: April 2019

Production reference: 1250419

Published by Packt Publishing Ltd.
Livery Place
35 Livery Street
Birmingham
B3 2PB, UK.

ISBN 978-1-78995-531-6

www.packtpub.com

To Mr. G. and Chiz, and to all teachers who support students in following unusual paths.

`mapt.io`

Mapt is an online digital library that gives you full access to over 5,000 books and videos, as well as industry leading tools to help you plan your personal development and advance your career. For more information, please visit our website.

Why subscribe?

- Spend less time learning and more time coding with practical eBooks and Videos from over 4,000 industry professionals

- Improve your learning with Skill Plans built especially for you

- Get a free eBook or video every month

- Mapt is fully searchable

- Copy and paste, print, and bookmark content

Packt.com

Did you know that Packt offers eBook versions of every book published, with PDF and ePub files available? You can upgrade to the eBook version at `www.packt.com` and as a print book customer, you are entitled to a discount on the eBook copy. Get in touch with us at `customercare@packtpub.com` for more details.

At `www.packt.com`, you can also read a collection of free technical articles, sign up for a range of free newsletters, and receive exclusive discounts and offers on Packt books and eBooks.

Contributors

About the author

Edward L. Platt creates technology for communities and communities for technology. He is currently a researcher at the University of Michigan School of Information and the Center for the Study of Complex Systems. He has published research on large-scale collective action, social networks, and online communities. He was formerly a staff researcher at the MIT Center for Civic Media. He contributes to many free/open source software projects, including tools for media analysis, network science, and cooperative organizations. He has also done research on quantum computing and fault tolerance. He has an M.Math in Applied Mathematics from the University of Waterloo, as well as B.S degrees in both Computer Science and Physics from MIT.

Many thanks to Andy Brosius for sharing their life and family with me, and for their incredible understanding and support while writing this book. Thanks to Persephone Hernandez-Vogt for their companionship and encouragement. Thanks to my editors at Packt, in particular Sandeep Mishra, for helping make this book a reality. Thanks to my Ph.D. advisor, Daniel Romero, for his mentorship and patience. And thanks to all of the NetworkX contributors.

About the reviewer

Nathan George is a data science professor at Regis University, with experience in manufacturing, neural networks, and Python and R for data science.

Packt is searching for authors like you

If you're interested in becoming an author for Packt, please visit authors.packtpub.com and apply today. We have worked with thousands of developers and tech professionals, just like you, to help them share their insight with the global tech community. You can make a general application, apply for a specific hot topic that we are recruiting an author for, or submit your own idea.

Table of Contents

Preface

Network science is becoming an increasingly valuable skill for both researchers and data scientists. Tools originally developed by sociologists and other researchers working with pen and paper have seen a resurgence as online platforms and social networks create huge datasets and advances in computer hardware make it feasible to analyze those data sets.

NetworkX is a free, open source Python package for network science. Python has become a popular choice for data scientists, with packages such as NumPy and pandas, making NetworkX a natural choice for augmenting data analysis with network-based techniques. Because NetworkX is written entirely in Python, it is easy to install across many different platforms. Other packages written in lower-level languages can sometimes provide better performance on very large networks, but can be difficult to install on some systems, and might not run at all on others. NetworkX is a great tool for learning network science and writing code that you can share with anyone.

Because NetworkX is free software, distributed under the Modified BSD License, anyone is free to use it, to look at the code, and to make improvements. As a result, NetworkX has a large and ever-growing set of features. And if it's missing something, you can always add it yourself rather than waiting for someone else to do it.

Who this book is for

I have tried to write this book for aspiring network scientists, managers who work with network scientists, and students from high school to Ph.D. level; anyone who wants to learn the basics of network science from the ground up. The only previous knowledge you will need is some familiarity with the Python programming language, or programming in general. I will avoid the mathematical details, instead focusing on the programming and applications. For the truly adventurous reader, the basic mathematics of networks are described in *Appendix*.

What this book covers

Chapter 1, *What is a Network?*, gives an overview of the history of network science and social network analysis, as well as introducing common types of networks and walking you through writing your first program with NetworkX.

Chapter 2, *Working with Networks in NetworkX*, describes simple, directed, and weighted networks, and how to work with them in NetworkX.

Chapter 3, *From Data to Networks*, describes functions for loading network data and for creating networks from scratch.

Chapter 4, *Affiliation Networks*, focuses on networks with two types of nodes (such as groups and group members) and shows how to work with these networks in NetworkX, as well as how to convert them to co-affiliation networks with just a single type of node.

Chapter 5, *The Small Scale—Nodes and Centrality*, shows how to use NetworkX to analyze network structure by looking at the properties of individual nodes and their connections.

Chapter 6, *The Big Picture—Describing Networks*, introduces several measures used to classify the structure of entire networks, and shows how these measures can differentiate between different types of real-world networks.

Chapter 7, *In-Between—Communities*, discusses medium-scale network structure, including community detection, clique detection, and k-cores.

Chapter 8, *Social Networks and Going Viral*, focuses on the special considerations that arise when network science is applied to social networks, as well as how the properties of social networks influence the spread of contagions such as disease or innovation.

Chapter 9, *Simulation and Analysis*, introduces several models used to generate networks based on underlying assumptions, as well as how to use agent-based models to simulate the evolution of a networked system.

Chapter 10, *Networks in Space and Time*, covers special considerations for network data associated with geographic locations and data that changes over time.

Chapter 11, *Visualization*, describes several visualization functions provided by NetworkX, as well as how to use them to visualize network information effectively.

Chapter 12, *Conclusion*, summarizes the lessons learned throughout this book, and provides resources for pursuing more advanced topics in network science.

To get the most out of this book

This book assumes very little previous knowledge—only a familiarity with the fundamentals of programming. Knowledge of the Python programming language is helpful for understanding the examples, but for readers only familiar with other programming languages, the code comments and descriptions should not be too difficult to understand.

The examples in this book can be run in any Python environment with access to the required libraries, but Jupyter Lab is recommended and offers several benefits. Jupyter Lab is an interactive programming environment for Python and other languages. Jupyter Lab runs in a web browser and makes it possible to visualize outputs along with the code, as well as to easily modify and re-run chunks of code.

Download the example code files

You can download the example code files for this book from your account at www.packt.com. If you purchased this book elsewhere, you can visit www.packt.com/support and register to have the files emailed directly to you.

You can download the code files by following these steps:

1. Log in or register at www.packt.com.
2. Select the **SUPPORT** tab.
3. Click on **Code Downloads & Errata**.
4. Enter the name of the book in the **Search** box and follow the onscreen instructions.

Once the file is downloaded, please make sure that you unzip or extract the folder using the latest version of:

- WinRAR/7-Zip for Windows
- Zipeg/iZip/UnRarX for Mac
- 7-Zip/PeaZip for Linux

The code bundle for the book is also hosted on GitHub at https://github.com/PacktPublishing/Network-Science-with-Python-and-NetworkX-Quick-Start-Guide. In case there's an update to the code, it will be updated on the existing GitHub repository.

We also have other code bundles from our rich catalog of books and videos available at https://github.com/PacktPublishing/. Check them out!

Conventions used

There are a number of text conventions used throughout this book.

`CodeInText`: Indicates code words in text, database table names, folder names, filenames, file extensions, pathnames, dummy URLs, user input, and Twitter handles. Here is an example: "Mount the downloaded `WebStorm-10*.dmg` disk image file as another disk in your system."

A block of code is set as follows:

```
G_karate = nx.karate_club_graph()
mr_hi = 0
john_a = 33
```

When code produces text output, that text output is set in bold:

```
list(nx.all_shortest_paths(G_karate, mr_hi, john_a))
[[0, 8, 33], [0, 13, 33], [0, 19, 33], [0, 31, 33]]
```

Bold: Indicates a new term or an important word. For example: "Statements that refer to themselves are called *self-referential*."

Warnings or important notes appear like this.

Tips and tricks appear like this.

Get in touch

Feedback from our readers is always welcome.

General feedback: If you have questions about any aspect of this book, mention the book title in the subject of your message and email us at `customercare@packtpub.com`.

Errata: Although we have taken every care to ensure the accuracy of our content, mistakes do happen. If you have found a mistake in this book, we would be grateful if you would report this to us. Please visit `www.packt.com/submit-errata`, selecting your book, clicking on the Errata Submission Form link, and entering the details.

Piracy: If you come across any illegal copies of our works in any form on the Internet, we would be grateful if you would provide us with the location address or website name. Please contact us at copyright@packt.com with a link to the material.

If you are interested in becoming an author: If there is a topic that you have expertise in and you are interested in either writing or contributing to a book, please visit authors.packtpub.com.

Reviews

Please leave a review. Once you have read and used this book, why not leave a review on the site that you purchased it from? Potential readers can then see and use your unbiased opinion to make purchase decisions, we at Packt can understand what you think about our products, and our authors can see your feedback on their book. Thank you!

For more information about Packt, please visit packt.com.

1
What is a Network?

In 1736, a Swiss mathematician pondered routes for a sightseeing trip along the Pregel River in Königsberg. In 1880, an Italian painter turned zoologist sought to settle a hotly-contested controversy: whether or not birds protect crops by reducing insect populations. In 1932, the superintendent of a girls' reformatory school in Hudson, New York, hired a sociologist to investigate the cause of a recent wave of runaways. In 1955, a U.S. Army General and a mathematician developed a technique for identifying bottlenecks in the Soviet railway system. And, in 1998, two mathematicians in Ithaca, New York tried to figure out (among other things) why exactly all movie stars seem to be connected by Kevin Bacon.

These puzzles, taking place at different times and different places, might, at first glance, appear unrelated. But they have one thing in common: they all revolve around relationships – between people, between places, or between species – and they were all solved using the science of relationships, which has come to be known as **network science**. Interest in network science has grown considerably in recent years, as online social network platforms, such as Facebook, Twitter, WeChat, and Mastodon, have become increasingly popular.

This book covers the fundamental concepts of network science, as well as how to put them into practice using the Python-based NetworkX package. Part I (Chapter 1, *What is a Network?*, to Chapter 4, *Affiliation Networks*) introduces the concept of a network, as well as how to build, manipulate, and visualize networks in NetworkX. Part II (Chapter 5, *The Small Scale – Nodes and Centrality*, to Chapter 7, *In-Between – Communities*) demonstrates how to analyze network structure at various scales. Part III (Chapter 8, *Social Networks and Going Viral*, to Chapter 11, *Visualization*) applies network science to understanding complex systems using modeling, simulation, and visualization. In this introductory chapter, you'll learn some of the history of network science and the differences between common types of networks. You'll also see examples of different ways that relationships in a network can be interpreted. Finally, you'll get to build and visualize your first network using NetworkX!

In this chapter, we will cover the following topics:

- **Network science**: Learn the history of the study of networks.
- **What is a network?**: Understand the fundamental concepts of network science.
- **What is NetworkX?**: Getting familiar with the NetworkX Python package.
- **Types of networks**: Meet common variants of networks, and understand their applications.
- **Your first network in NetworkX**: Try a simple example.

Network science

The origins of network science trace back to many different fields. For the most part, researchers in these fields developed the tools and methods of network science without much knowledge of how it was being applied in other fields. It may seem astonishing that scientists working independently in very different fields could develop tools and techniques similar enough to now be considered a single field.

How did this happen? The answer lies in one insight: sometimes, it is useful to study the relationships between things without worrying about the specifics of what those things are. Network scientists didn't study networks for their own sake* – they studied networks in order to better understand people, animal species, atoms, and so on. (* Except for mathematicians. We like to think about weird abstract concepts such as networks just for fun.)

When the specifics of the people/species/atoms being studied were abstracted away, seemingly different problems suddenly became very similar. And that's the power of network science; it provides a general language to talk about relationships and connections, allowing discoveries about one thing to be translated into useful information about many other types of things.

The history of network science

The earliest work recognizable as network science came from the branch of mathematics known as **graph theory**. Graph theory originated with Leonhard Euler's 1736 solution (Euler, 1953) to the seven bridges problem. At the time, the city of Königsberg, Prussia (now Kaliningrad, Russia) had seven bridges connecting the banks of the Pregel River to two islands (pictured as follows). It was not known whether it was possible to find a path through the city that crossed every bridge exactly once. Euler showed that it was impossible, and he did so using new methods that became the basis for graph theory, and later for network science.

 Leonhard Euler was a prolific 18th century mathematician. His surname is pronounced "oiler" (and his work does indeed lubricate the gears of modern mathematics). He is perhaps best remembered by his namesake: Euler's number, $e \approx 2.7$ (which, confusingly, was discovered by Jacob Bernoulli):

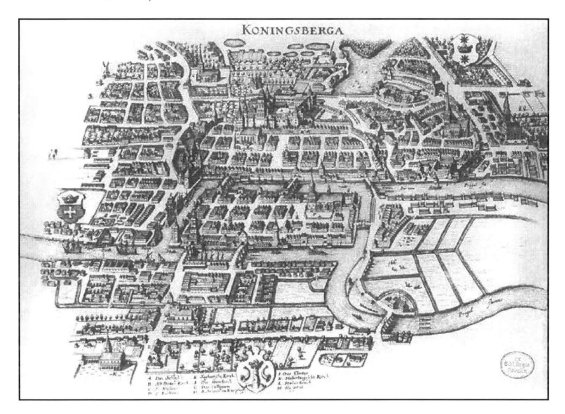

Seventeenth-century Königsberg and its seven bridges

The study of networks also has a rich history in sociology. The sociologists, Jacob L. Moreno and Helen Hall Jennings proposed tools for the quantitative study of interpersonal relationships, which they called **sociometry** (Moreno & Jennings, 1934). These tools included the **sociogram**, a graphical representation of social networks very similar to the type of network diagrams currently in use.

When Moreno was hired by Fannie French Morse, superintendent of the New York Training School for Girls, to investigate a wave of runaways, it was sociograms that allowed him to visualize and communicate the nature of the social forces driving the runaways. Many of the tools used in modern network science—centrality, affiliation networks, community detection, and others—come from sociology. Over the past several decades, sociometry has branched into social network analysis, a rich and active subfield within network science.

 Sociology is the science concerned with how individuals and their interactions produce institutions and societies. Networks are used in sociology to represent and quantify the relationships between individuals.

Various other fields have found it useful to study network structure, and have shared their tools and findings with each other as part of the interdisciplinary **complex systems** community. Ecologists study food webs—relationships between predator and prey species. Biologists study networks of interactions between genes. Physicists study magnetic interactions between neighboring atoms in crystals. All of these fields are doing exciting work with network science.

 Complex systems are those that arise from the interactions of simpler components, for example, traffic from cars, stock markets from stock trades, and ecologies from species. Networks are used to analyze and study the interrelationships between components.

And then, of course, there's the internet. The internet itself is literally a network—computers and routers connected to each other by copper wire, fiber optic cables, and so on. But, on top of that, the content on the internet is also networked. Links between web pages form networks, and online social networks allow people to interact by friending or following each other. The Google search engine was founded on the PageRank algorithm (Page et al., 1999), a network-science-based approach to identifying popular websites. Online social networks typically make money by selling advertising space, and using network science to show ads to the people most likely to click on them. If you see a picture of a cute cat online, you can use network science to understand how the picture got to your computer screen, how the picture connects you with your friends, and what the picture tells you about other sites you might like to visit.

Online activity leaves **digital trace** data—records of activity stored in logs and databases. Digital trace data can often be used to construct networks of relationships between individuals. From these networks, it is surprisingly easy to predict many things, such as purchasing preferences (Zhang & Pennacchiotti, 2013), political ideology (Cohen & Ruths, 2013), and even sexual orientation (Jernigan & Mistree, 2009). The powerful techniques available for such data raises both exciting possibilities and complex ethical considerations.

Network science today

With its interdisciplinary nature, network science draws practitioners from a wide variety of backgrounds. At the time of writing this book, only a handful of universities offer programs dedicated to network science, so network scientists tend to be self-taught, or trained as sociologists, physicists, ecologists, and so on. My own path to network science was similarly convoluted. Once an aspiring physicist, I came to realize I cared more about people than atoms, and left grad school to work on technology for civic organizing. When I eventually came across network science, I was excited to find that it was a powerful tool for understanding group behavior, and that the skills I'd learned from physics transferred directly to network science. Since then, I have been using network science to better understand how groups can organize and collaborate more effectively. Whatever your background, network science is a place where everyone fits in because no one fits in.

Network science has experienced rapid growth in recent years, in part due to the popularity of online social networks, digital trace data, and tools such as NetworkX. Once scattered across many different fields, universities are now creating research centers and Ph.D. programs specifically dedicated to network science. Companies have rushed to hire data scientists, including network scientists. There has never been a better time to explore the delightful world of network data.

What is a network?

If you walk down into the Kendall Square subway station in Cambridge, Massachusetts, through the turnstiles and past the Paul Matisse art installation, you will see a common feature of all subways: a map.

If you have ever used a subway map, you know that they are not quite like other maps, which tend to be concerned with details like distance and terrain. Subway maps leave all that out, showing you the bare minimum you need to know to get from one place to another: which stations are connected to each other.

When you're using a subway, it doesn't matter how long a stretch of track is, what exact direction it goes in, or even whether it is above ground, underground, or under water. All you have to do is get on at one station and get off at another, possibly with some transfers between the two. Such a map is an excellent example of the types of networks used by network scientists.

Nodes and edges

In network science, a network is simply a set of things and the connections between them. The things are called **nodes**, and the connections are called **edges**. Nodes are really just placeholders for any type of thing that can have a connection or relationship, such as subway stations, people, or atoms. Similarly, edges are placeholders for connections or relationships, such as subway tracks, friendships, or molecular bonds. Just like the subway map, representing a system as a network strips away a lot of information, making it possible to focus just on the structure.

 Sometimes, you might see nodes called vertices, or edges called links. Mathematicians like vertices and edges, while computer scientists prefer nodes and links. NetworkX uses nodes and edges (perhaps as a compromise?), so I will use that terminology in this book.

Visualizing networks

Networks are often visualized by drawing a dot or circle for each node and a line for each edge, as in the following diagram:

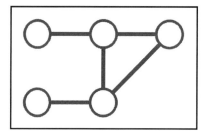

Example network with five nodes

Looking at the network in this diagram, you might as yourself where to draw the nodes. The answer is wherever you want! (Although technically possible, it might be advisable to avoid hot surfaces, the mouths of large predatory animals, and/or important historical documents.) Because networks are meant to focus on structure and connectivity, there are many ways to draw the same network. Nodes can be drawn anywhere. Edges can be straight or squiggly, long or short. Edges can even cross, but that should never be interpreted as being connected to each other!

The same network can be drawn in many other ways, as shown in the following diagram. The nodes have been labelled with letters to make it easier to compare between different network diagrams. Regardless of which diagram you look at, any particular node will be connected to the same set of other nodes. While different ways of drawing the same network are equally correct, some may be helpful at highlighting particular features of the network. Chapter 11, *Visualization*, describes common approaches to visualizing networks and their various applications:

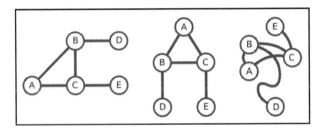

Equivalent networks

What is NetworkX?

Remember NetworkX? This is a book about NetworkX. NetworkX is a Python package for modeling, analyzing, and visualizing networks. It provides classes to represent several types of networks and implementations of many of the algorithms used in network science. NetworkX is relatively easy to install and use, and has much of the functionality built-in, so it is ideal for learning network science and performing analyses on small or medium sized networks. There is excellent documentation available on the project website at https://networkx.github.io/.

At the time of writing, NetworkX is in version 2.3. While many things are exactly the same between 1.x versions and 2.x, some basic functionality has changed, so documentation and books relating to older versions may no longer be accurate. This book assumes versions at or above 2.3, so all examples here should work with recent versions of NetworkX.

NetworkX is **Free and Open Source Software** (**FOSS**). That means that the source code is available to read, modify, and redistribute (under certain conditions). The code itself is available at `https://github.com/networkx/networkx`. In addition to the original authors and project maintainers, NetworkX has been written by a community of dozens of contributors. If you have an idea for a new feature or a way to improve the software, you can write it yourself and contribute it back to the community.

When contributing to FOSS projects, it is good etiquette to read the contributor guidelines. These guidelines help project contributors collaborate effectively, avoid conflicting changes, and ensure reliability of the software.

Types of networks

The networks presented in this chapter so far have just the bare essentials. These networks are called simple networks because, well, they are simple. In NetworkX, simple networks are represented by the `Graph` class, described in detail in `Chapter 2`, *Working with Networks in NetworkX*.

The name `Graph` comes from the term used in math to describe networks. You'd think it would mean a picture or drawing, but in this case, it just means a network. Mathematicians often use everyday words in very specific ways that are quite different from their everyday meanings, for example, "graph", "bundle", "ring", and "clearly".

Directed networks

Sometimes, it helps to add just a little more detail to a network. The edges we've seen so far don't have any sense of *coming from* or *going to*; they are simply connections between two nodes, so they are called **symmetric** or **undirected**.

Imagine a network that represents a system of roads (edges) and intersections (nodes). A network with undirected edges would be a good representation, until you came across a one-way street. An undirected edge suggests that you can travel in either direction equally well, while in reality, driving against traffic is likely to be a rather different experience from driving with it.

When direction matters, a network is called **directed**. In a directed network, each edge has a **source** node and a **target** node. Typically, the edge represents a flow of some kind, for example, traffic, from the source to the target. But what if not all connections are one-way? Easy! Two-way connections are made by combining two directed edges going in opposite directions. In directed networks, edges are drawn with arrows pointing toward the target, as shown in the following diagram. In NetworkX, directed networks are represented by the DiGraph class, also described in Chapter 2, *Working with Networks in NetworkX*:

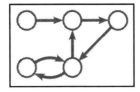

Example of a directed network

Weighted networks

Returning to the case of undirected networks, sometimes, not all edges are created equal. For example, in a network representing a city's water distribution system, the edges could represent a series of tubes that carry the water from one place to another. Some of these might have greater capacity than others. When edges can have different strengths, the network is called **weighted**, and the strength is quantified by a number called the **weight**. Both directed and undirected networks can be weighted. An example of a weighted network is shown in the following diagram. When visualizing a network, edge weights are often indicated by varying the thickness or opacity of the edge. Edge weights can be used to represent many different types of attributes. The most common ones are described in the next section:

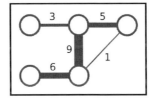

Example of a weighted network

Understanding edges

Edges represent the connections and relationships that make a network. The edges and their weights can have different interpretations, depending on what the network represents. Some common interpretations include the following:

- Friendships
- Flows
- Similarity
- Distance

Social networks

In social networks, edges most often represent friendship or other interpersonal relationships. Edge weights then represent the strength of the friendship, for example, time spent together, messages exchanged, or the number of common interests.

Flow networks

Flow networks describe the movement of something (people, information, fluid, and so on) from place to place. Edge weights might represent capacity—the maximum amount that can be transported between two nodes—or the actual amount that has traveled through/across the connection.

Similarity networks

In similarity networks, connections are less literal and more abstract. Edge weights correspond to how similar two nodes are, often with zero being not at all, and one being identical. For example, one type of similarity between different people could be calculated by taking their top-10 favorite online cat videos and using the fraction of videos that appear for both people. In this case, the edge weight doesn't have anything to do with whether two people have any kind of relationship. It's quite possible to have an edge with a very high weight connecting two individuals who have never even met!

Spatial networks

Edges can also represent distance (or closeness), especially when nodes represent locations in space. When using edge weights to represent distance, the distance of an entire trip can be calculated by adding together all of the edge weights along a path. Using edge weights to represent distance can sometimes be confusing because a larger number means a weaker connection, and non-existent edges are actually edges with an infinite weight. Sometimes, it can be more intuitive to use a measure of closeness, such as the reciprocal of the distance, although that can complicate working with paths across many edges.

The previous examples cover many of the common applications of networks, but they are by no means exhaustive. Whenever a group of things can have any type of relationship or connection with each other, it is possible to capture the structure of those connections using a network.

Your first network in NetworkX

Now, let's create and visualize a small network using NetworkX! For the code in this book, you will need Python 3.4 or higher and NetworkX 2.2 or greater. I also highly recommend Jupyter Lab as an interactive Python environment. The code in this book is available as Jupyter notebooks at `https://github.com/PacktPublishing/Network-Science-with-Python-and-NetworkX-Quick-Start-Guide`.

 The code in this book was written using NetworkX 2.3. At time of writing, NetworkX 2.3 is available but has not been officially released. All of the examples will work with NetworkX 2.2, but may have minor differences in node color and formatting.

The following example creates an undirected, unweighted network, adds edges and nodes, and then generates a visualization. Other types of networks will be discussed in Chapter 2, *Working with Networks in NetworkX*. First, we import the `networkx` package. In this book, I will use the convention of importing the library with the alias `nx`:

```
import networkx as nx
```

Next, we create a `Graph` object, representing an undirected network, given as follows:

```
G = nx.Graph()
```

Now that the graph exists, we can add nodes one at a time with the `add_node()` method, or all at once with `add_nodes_from()`. When adding nodes to a network, each node has to have a unique ID. The ID can be a number, a string, or a tuple. In fact, you can use any Python object as an ID, as long as it has a __hash__() method defined. For this example, we'll use letters as node IDs, shown as follows:

```
G.add_node('A')
G.add_nodes_from(['B', 'C'])
```

Similarly, edges can be added one at a time with `add_edge()`, or all at once with `add_edges_from()`, shown as follows:

```
G.add_edge('A', 'B')
G.add_edges_from([('B', 'C'), ('A', 'C')])
```

So far, the A, B, and C nodes, as well as the edges connecting them, have been added. The following code draws a simple visualization of the network:

```
plt.figure(figsize=(7.5, 7.5))
nx.draw_networkx(G)
plt.show()
```

In the preceding code, `figure()` is used to create a 7.5 by 7.5 inch figure, which will hold the visualization. The `draw_networkx()` function uses the `Graph` object G to produce a visualization. The `show()` function renders the visualization, but can be omitted if you are running the examples in Jupyter Lab. The visualization should appear similar to the following:

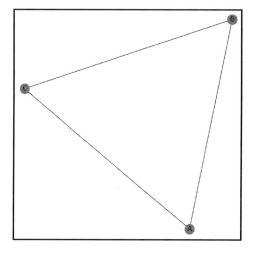

Output of draw_networkx()

NetworkX has several functions for visualizing networks, each of which allows you to customize the visualization style. Some of these functions and parameters are discussed over the remaining chapters, in particular Chapter 11, *Visualization*.

Your visualization may look slightly different from the one shown previously. This is because visualizations in NetworkX sometimes use randomized algorithms. The randomized algorithms can be configured to produce the same output each time by setting the **random seed**. The following code sets the random seeds used by NetworkX (this code will also appear at the beginning of the example code for all future chapters):

```
import random
from numpy import random as nprand
seed = hash("Network Science in Python") % 2**32
nprand.seed(seed)
random.seed(seed)
```

 The pyplot figure() function is used in the preceding code to set the size of the visualization figure, but doing that each time can be tedious. Instead, it is possible to set the default figure size as follows:

```
plt.rcParams.update({'figure.figsize': (7.5, 7.5)})
```

Nodes can also be added using a nifty shortcut. If you try to add an edge referring to a node ID that isn't in the network, NetworkX will automatically add the node! So, in practice, you won't often need to call add_node() directly. The following code adds nodes and edges so that the network matches the example network from earlier and creates a new visualization:

```
G.add_edges_from([('B', 'D'), ('C', 'E')])
nx.draw_networkx(G)
```

The `draw_networkx()` function now produces a visualization including the new D and E nodes:

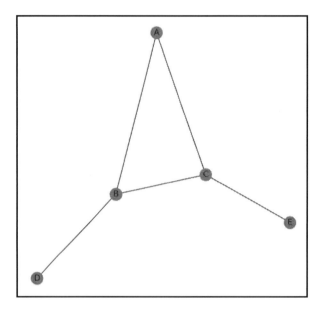

Output of draw_networkx() after adding nodes

Summary

From the bridges of 17th century Königsberg to the internet, network science emerged from a diverse range of fields, all seeking to quantify and study relationships of some kind. The networks in network science model relationships as edges between nodes, which can represent anything from a species of flower, to an atom in a crystal, to an individual in a society. To quantify properties of relationships, edges can be directed and/or weighted. NetworkX provides Python classes and functions to create and manipulate such networks with ease. By now, you should have a sense of the types of problems network science and NetworkX can solve. The following chapters will cover various applications of network science as well as related features of NetworkX, with examples of how they can be applied to real datasets.

References

The following is a list of resources that you can consider to get further knowledge:

- Cohen, R., & Ruths, D. (2013). Classifying political orientation on Twitter: It's not easy!. In *Seventh International AAAI Conference on Weblogs and Social Media*.
- Euler, L. (1953). Leonhard Euler and the Königsberg bridges. Scientific American, 189(1).
- Jernigan, C., & Mistree, B. F. (2009). Gaydar: Facebook friendships expose sexual orientation. *First Monday*, 14(10).
- Moreno, J. L., & Jennings, H. H. (1934). Who Shall Survive? Nervous and Mental Disease.
- Page, L., Brin, S., Motwani, R., & Winograd, T. (1999). *The PageRank citation ranking: Bringing order to the web*. Stanford InfoLab.
- Zhang, Y., & Pennacchiotti, M. (2013, May). Predicting purchase behaviors from social media. In *Proceedings of the 22nd international conference on World Wide Web*. ACM.

2
Working with Networks in NetworkX

The basic features of NetworkX are contained in several Python classes that represent different types of networks. In particular, this chapter discusses `Graph`, `DiGraph`, `MultiGraph`, and `MultiDiGraph`. These classes can be used to represent, analyze, and visualize most networks. In this chapter, you will learn to use these classes to work with real-world network data in NetworkX. The code examples in this and future chapters will assume that you have already imported the `networkx` package.

In this chapter, we will cover the following topics:

- **The Graph class**: Understand the properties of undirected networks and how they are represented using the NetworkX `Graph` class.
- **Attributes**: How to associate data with nodes and edges.
- **Edge weights**: Learn how to quantify connection strength, and annotate edges with that information.
- **The DiGraph class**: Understand the properties of directed networks and how they are represented using the NetworkX `DiGraph` class.
- **The MultiGraph and MultiDiGraph classes**: Learn about networks with parallel edges.

The Graph class – undirected networks

In NetworkX, the `Graph` class is used to represent undirected networks and analyze their structure. The previous chapter showed how to create a network from scratch by adding nodes and edges. This section will instead use one of the ready-made networks available in NetworkX: Zachary's karate club (Zachary, 1977).

This network represents the friendships (edges) between members (nodes) of a karate club studied between 1970 and 1972. This particular karate club has long been of interest to sociologists and network scientists, because it eventually split into two different clubs after a disagreement between the instructor and the club president (this might explain why there aren't any famous studies of conflict resolution clubs). In the original study, Zachary used the network structure to predict which members would join which of the two clubs with near-perfect accuracy! Specifically, he used the minimum-cut algorithm discussed in Chapter 7, *In-Between – Communities*.

The karate club network can be created and visualized using the karate_club_graph() function given as follows:

```
G = nx.karate_club_graph()
karate_pos = nx.spring_layout(G, k=0.3)
nx.draw_networkx(G, karate_pos)
```

The preceding code stores the karate club network in G. The visualization layout is then pre-calculated using spring_layout() and stored in karate_pos, which will allow us to reuse the layout throughout the chapter. Different layout methods are discussed in detail in Chapter 11, *Visualization*, but for now, all you need to know is that spring_layout() tries to place nodes closer together if they are connected by an edge. Finally, the call to draw_networkx() creates the following visualization:

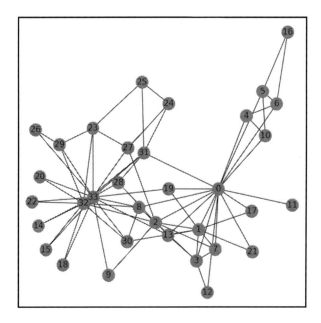

The Zachary karate club network

The `Graph` class offers many ways to interact with nodes and edges. The nodes and edges in a `Graph` class can be accessed using its `nodes` and `edges` attributes. These attributes are iterables and can be used to iterate over nodes and edges, or converted to a `list` of node IDs and edges, demonstrated as follows:

```
list(G.nodes)
[0, 1, 2, ...]

list(G.edges)
[(0, 1), (0, 2), (0, 3), ...]
```

Another simple way to interact with a network is to check whether a particular node is present. In Zachary's paper, the node with the `0` ID was identified as the club instructor, *Mr. Hi* (a pseudonym). It's easy to confirm that Mr. Hi's node is part of the network using the Python `in` operator, or the `Graph` class's `has_node()` method, given as follows:

```
mr_hi = 0
mr_hi in G
True

G.has_node(mr_hi)
True
```

These statements evaluate to `True` because `G` contains a node with an ID matching the given value. If the given value doesn't match any of the node IDs, the statement evaluates to `False` as follows:

```
wild_goose = 1337
wild_goose in G
False

G.has_node(wild_goose)
False
```

Now that you know that Mr. Hi is part of the network, you can examine his friendships. Each edge connected to Mr. Hi's node represents one of his friendships. The nodes on the other end of these edges represent his friends. In general, the set of nodes that are connected to a particular node by an edge are called that node's **neighbors** and can be found using the `neighbors()` method of the `Graph` class. The `neighbors()` method returns an iterator, which is handy for most uses, but if you just want to see the neighbors, you can use the `list()` constructor:

```
list(G.neighbors(mr_hi))
[1, 2, 3, 4, 5, 6, 7, 8, 10, 11, 12, 13, 17, 19, 21, 31]
```

So, Mr. Hi has 16 friends, represented by the preceding node IDs. You can test whether a given edge exists using either the Python `in` operator or the `Graph` class's `has_edge()` method. If you just want to know whether Mr. Hi is friends with a particular club member (say node ID 1), you can use the following code:

```
member_id = 1
(mr_hi, member_id) in G.edges
True

G.has_edge(mr_hi, member_id)
True
```

The president of the karate club, nicknamed *John A.*, is represented by ID 33. The following code checks whether he and Mr. Hi are friends:

```
john_a = 33
(mr_hi, john_a) in G.edges
False
G.has_edge(mr_hi, john_a)
False
```

The previous result tells us that the club president and the instructor were not friends. Perhaps that played a role in the demise of the club...

Adding attributes to nodes and edges

In the last chapter, I said that networks were entirely defined by the number of nodes and which nodes were connected. I lied. Kind of. Now that we're all a little older and wiser than we were in `Chapter 1`, *What is a Network?*, I can tell you the whole truth: sometimes, network nodes and edges are annotated with additional information. In the `Graph` class, each node and edge can have a set of **attributes** to store this additional information. Attributes can simply be a convenient place to store information related to the nodes and edges, or they can be used by visualizations and network algorithms.

The `Graph` class allows you to add any number of attributes to a node. For a `G`, network, each node's attributes are stored in the dict at `G.nodes[v]`, where `v` is the node's ID. In the karate club example, the club members eventually split into two separate clubs. We can add an attribute to each node to describe which splinter club the corresponding member joined after the original club disbanded. The club joined by member `i` is given by the ith element of the following list:

```
member_club = [
    0, 0, 0, 0, 0, 0, 0, 0, 1, 1,
    0, 0, 0, 0, 1, 1, 0, 0, 1, 0,
    1, 0, 1, 1, 1, 1, 1, 1, 1, 1,
    1, 1, 1, 1]
```

This information can be added by iterating over all the node IDs and setting the node attribute based on the value in `member_club`, as follows:

```
for node_id in G.nodes:
    G.nodes[node_id]["club"] = member_club[node_id]
```

Attributes can also be added automatically when a new node is added by passing keyword arguments to `add_node()` after the node ID as follows:

```
G.add_node(11, club=0)
```

Now that the club attribute has been set for all the nodes, it's possible to check the value of that attribute for individual nodes, shown as follows:

```
G.nodes[mr_hi]
{'club': 0}
```

```
G.nodes[john_a]
{'club': 1}
```

It looks like Mr. Hi and John A really don't get along very well and ended up joining different clubs. We can visualize these different clubs by using different colors. The list of node colors can be created by iterating through the nodes and assigning a color based on their `club` attribute. That list can then be passed to the `draw_networkx()` function as follows:

```
node_colors = [
    '#1f78b4' if G.nodes[v]["club"] == 0
    else '#33a02c' for v in G]
nx.draw_networkx(G, karate_pos, label=True, node_color=node_color)
```

In the preceding code, a color is stored in the `node_colors` list for each node, and passed to `draw_networkx()`, which will produce the following:

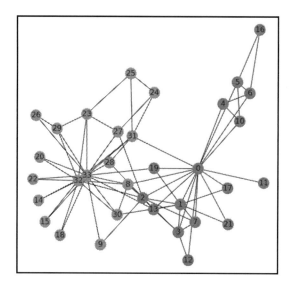

The Zachary network after splitting into two clubs

Adding attributes to edges works much like it does for nodes. In a `G` network, an edge's attributes are stored in the dict at `G.edges[v, w]`, where `v` and `w` are the node IDs of the edge endpoints. Note that since the `Graph` class represents an undirected network, these attributes can also be accessed at `G.edges[w, v]`. You might think that you'd need to update both separately (if you're prone to anxiety), but NetworkX takes care of that for you.

Some of the edges in the karate club network connect members who joined the same splinter club, while other edges connect members from different splinter clubs. This information can be stored in the `Graph` class using edge attributes. To do so, iterate through all the edges, and check whether the edge endpoints have the same `club` attribute. In this example, I create an attribute called `internal` to represent whether an edge is internal to a single splinter club. This can be done using the following code:

```
# Iterate through all edges
for v, w in G.edges:
    # Compare `club` property of edge endpoints
    # Set edge `internal` property to True if they match
    if G.nodes[v]["club"] == G.nodes[w]["club"]:
        G.edges[v, w]["internal"] = True
    else:
        G.edges[v, w]["internal"] = False
```

The two types of edges could also be visualized with color, but we'll need color in the next section, so let's use solid lines for internal edges and dashed lines for external ones instead. The internal and external edges can be found by iterating through the edges and checking the `internal` attribute. Note that rather than using the individual node IDs v and w, this example references edges using a single e variable, which contains a 2-tuple of node IDs, given as follows:

```
internal = [e for e in G.edges if G.edges[e]["internal"]]
external = [e for e in G.edges if ~G.edges[e]["internal"]]
```

NetworkX can only draw one line style at a time, so multiple line styles requires nodes, edges, and labels to be drawn separately. While doing so takes more code, it gives more control over the final output. First, we draw the nodes and node labels, specifying node colors using the `node_color` parameter:

```
# Draw nodes and node labels
nx.draw_networkx_nodes(G, karate_pos, node_color=node_color)
nx.draw_networkx_labels(G, karate_pos)
```

Next, we draw the internal and external edges separately, using the `style` parameter to draw the external edges as dashed lines:

```
# Draw internal edges as solid lines
nx.draw_networkx_edges(G, karate_pos, edgelist=internal)
# Draw external edges as dashed lines
nx.draw_networkx_edges(G, karate_pos, edgelist=external, style="dashed")
```

The preceding code will produce the following:

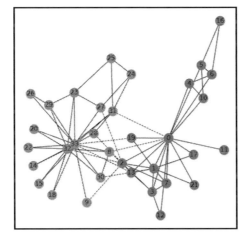

Internal and external edges in the Zachary network

Adding edge weights

So far, all of the edges in this chapter have been unweighted, but the `Graph` class also supports weighted edges. Edge weights are handy when connections can have different strengths and when there is a way to quantify the strength of a connection; for example, how often two friends talk to each other, the volume of fluid a pipe can transport, or the number of direct flights between two cities.

The karate club network doesn't have any additional information about the strength of the edges, but there are relevant properties of those edges that can be calculated, such as the **tie strength**. Tie strength increases with the number of neighbors that two nodes have in common. It is motivated by the observation that closer friends tend to have more friends in common, and it can often reveal insight into the structure of a social network. The following code calculates the tie strength using the `neighbors()` method to find node neighbors, and Python sets to compute the number of neighbors in common:

```
def tie_strength(G, v, w):
    # Get neighbors of nodes v and w in G
    v_neighbors = set(G.neighbors(v))
    w_neighbors = set(G.neighbors(w))
    # Return size of the set intersection
    return 1 + len(v_neighbors & w_neighbors)
```

Here, we've defined the tie strength as the number of common neighbors plus one. Why plus one? A weight of zero conventionally means no edge, so without the extra one, edges between nodes without common neighbors wouldn't count as edges.

Curious readers might wonder if there's a theoretical interpretation of that extra one. Well, if you and a friend don't have any friends in common, there's still one of their friends you're pretty well-acquainted with—yourself! So, the bonus term can be interpreted as coming from the edge itself. The weights are also stored in a list, which will be necessary momentarily.

In NetworkX, any edge attribute can be used as a weight. In the following example, the weight is just called `weight`, and is set to the tie strength:

```
# Calculate weight for each edge
for v, w in G.edges:
    G.edges[v, w]["weight"] = tie_strength(G, v, w)
# Store weights in a list
    edge_weights = [G.edges[v, w]["weight"] for v, w in G.edges]
```

The edge weights can be passed to `spring_layout()` in order to push strongly connected nodes even closer together, shown as follows:

```
weighted_pos = nx.spring_layout(G, pos=karate_pos, k=0.3, weight="weight")
```

By specifying the `pos` parameter of `spring_layout()`, `karate_pos` is used as the starting point of the new layout. Putting all of this together, the following code visualizes the weighted network:

```
# Draw network with edge color determined by weight
nx.draw_networkx(
    G, weighted_pos, width=8, node_color=node_color,
    edge_color=edge_weights, edge_cmap=plt.cm.Blues,
    edge_vmin=0, edge_vmax=6)

# Draw solid/dashed lines on top of internal/external edges
nx.draw_networkx_edges(
    G, weighted_pos, edgelist=internal, edge_color="gray")
nx.draw_networkx_edges(
    G, weighted_pos, edgelist=external, edge_color="gray", style="dashed")
```

To color the edges, the edge weights are passed to `draw_networkx()`. NetworkX then generates the colors by mapping them to colors using a color map. In this case, colors range from light blue (low weight) to dark blue (high weight). The weighted edges are drawn with a width of eight pixels to make them more visible. The edges are also drawn a second time on top of the first; this time, one pixel wide and either solid (for internal edges) or dashed (for external edges). The final visualization will resemble the following:

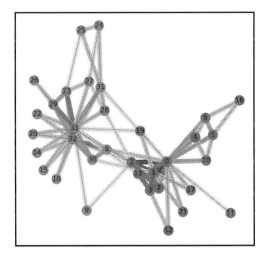

Tie strength in the Zachary network

The preceding screenshot makes it possible to visualize the strength of friendships, which splinter club each member joined, and which friendships were divided between clubs. While simple, the previous analysis of the karate club network enables some powerful insights. The friendships that were split between the two new clubs were typically weaker than others. Mr. Hi (node 0) and John A. (node 33) can both be seen in the center of their respective club, suggesting that they played an important role in the break-up of the original club and the formation of the new ones. If this analysis had been available to the original members of Zachary's karate club, perhaps it might have helped them strengthen the necessary relationships to keep the group together. This example has only scratched the surface of the features available in NetworkX, but hopefully it has demonstrated how powerful those features can be.

The DiGraph class – when direction matters

So far, all of the edges in this chapter have been undirected, with no difference between an edge from A to B, and an edge from B to A. But not all relationships in life are so symmetric. If an employee-boss relationship is described by an undirected edge, it suggests that the employee can fire the boss as easily as the other way around. While possibly good for workplace morale, such arrangements aren't the norm. NetworkX supports directed edges through the DiGraph (directed graph) class.

Many of the operations already described for the Graph class translate seamlessly to the DiGraph class. Iterating through nodes and edges, accessing attributes, and visualization are all exactly the same. But there are a few differences. This section will describe the most important of these differences.

This section will use another social network as an example: the friendships among adolescent students in a Dutch classroom, collected by Andrea Knecht (Knecht, 2008). Knecht's friendship network differs from Zachary's karate club because students were asked to list their friends, but there was no requirement that their friends listed them in return. In other words, the network is directed! The network data is available online and included along with the code for this book for convenience. The network can be loaded and visualized using the following code:

```
G = nx.read_gexf("data/knecht2008/klas12b-net-1.gexf")
student_pos = nx.spring_layout(G, k=1.5)
nx.draw_networkx(G, pos, arrowsize=20)
```

The `arrowsize` parameter of `draw_networkx()` is used to increase the size of arrows on directed edges, making them easier to see. This code produces the following visualization:

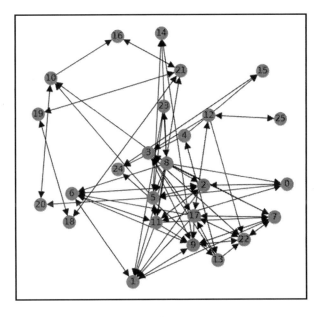

Knecht classroom friendship network

Notice that, in the preceding screenshot, some nodes are connected by a line with one arrowhead, which represents a single directed edge. Others are connected by a line with two arrowheads, representing two directed edges pointing in opposite directions.

In a directed network, there is not just one type of neighbor, there are two! A node can be connected to others by either incoming or outgoing edges (or both). Incoming edges connect a node to its **predecessors**, while outgoing edges connect a node to its **successors**. An imaginary mouse crawling along the network in the directions of the edges would move from predecessor to successor repeatedly (and probably become disappointed by the alarming lack of cheese in network science). The DiGraph class still has a `neighbors()` method, but it behaves a little differently, and, in fact, returns an iterator of successor nodes only. There is also a `successor()` method, which does exactly the same thing, but is a little more honest about it.

Similarly, the predecessors of a node can be found using the `predecessor()` method as follows:

```
list(G.neighbors(0))
[2, 5, 11]

list(G.successors(0))
[2, 5, 11]

list(G.predecessors(0))
[2, 11, 8]
```

Note that a neighbor can be both a predecessor and a successor, for example, 2 and 11 in the preceding code—they just don't need to be.

Node and edge attributes in a `DiGraph` class can be accessed exactly as they are in a `Graph` class, as well as in some new ways. While the `edges` attribute works perfectly well for `DiGraph`, the `in_edges` and `out_edges` attributes allow access to the same edges with the additional guarantee that, within each edge tuple, the first node is either the target (for `in_edges`) or the source (for `out_edges`).

Do you miss undirected networks yet? If so, `DiGraph` provides the `to_undirected()` method to create an undirected copy of itself, returning a `Graph`. By default, the new `Graph` will have an undirected edge between two nodes if a directed edge existed in **either** direction in the original `DiGraph`. However, if the `reciprocal` parameter is set to `True`, undirected edges will only be created if directed edges exist in **both** directions. Both options are visualized by the following code:

```
# Create undirected copies of G
G_either = G.to_undirected()
G_both = G.to_undirected(reciprocal=True)

# Set up a figure
plt.figure(figsize=(10,5))

# Draw G_either on left
plt.subplot(1, 2, 1)
nx.draw_networkx(G_either, student_pos)

# Draw G_both on right
plt.subplot(1, 2, 2)
nx.draw_networkx(G_both, student_pos)
```

The preceding code produces two visualizations, one which includes non-reciprocated edges (left) and one which includes only reciprocated edges (right):

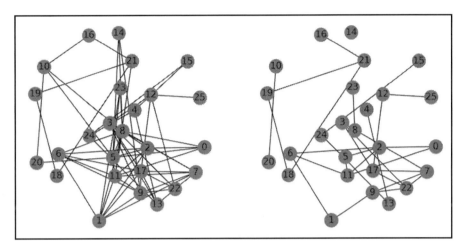

Transforming networks from directed to undirected

MultiGraph and MultiDiGraph – parallel edges

Meanwhile, in 18th-century Königsberg, both Graph and DiGraph fall short. Several of the bridges of Königsberg (discussed in Chapter 1, *What is a Network?*) connected the same two landmasses. In order to represent the bridges as a network, the nodes representing the land masses need to have multiple parallel edges, but the Graph class only allows one edge between a pair of nodes. For situations like this, NetworkX provides the MultiGraph and MultiDiGraph classes. For many applications, parallel edges can be combined into a single weighted edge, but when they can't, these classes can be used.

These MultiGraph and MultiDigraph classes work very much like Graph and DiGraph, but allow parallel edges. Any number of edges can be added between the same two endpoints. The following example reconstructs the Königsberg network and adds the name of each bridge as an edge attribute:

```
# The seven bridges of Königsberg
G = nx.MultiGraph()
G.add_edges_from([
    ("North Bank", "Kneiphof", {"bridge": "Krämerbrücke"}),
```

```
        ("North Bank", "Kneiphof", {"bridge": "Schmiedebrücke"}),
        ("North Bank", "Lomse",    {"bridge": "Holzbrücke"}),
        ("Lomse",      "Kneiphof", {"bridge": "Dombrücke"}),
        ("South Bank", "Kneiphof", {"bridge": "Grüne Brücke"}),
        ("South Bank", "Kneiphof", {"bridge": "Köttelbrücke"}),
        ("South Bank", "Lomse",    {"bridge": "Hohe Brücke"})
    ])
```

But now, if we want to look up the name of the bridge between the north bank and Kneiphof, NetworkX needs a way to know which one! Behind the scenes, NetworkX has assigned each edge a unique ID, which is stored in addition to its endpoints and data. Edges are now represented by three tuples, with the first two elements containing node IDs and the third containing the edge ID as follows:

```
list(G.edges)[0]
('North Bank', 'Kneiphof', 0)

G.edges['North Bank', 'Kneiphof', 0]
{'bridge': 'Krämerbrücke'}
```

Summary

All networks are composed of nodes and edges, but different systems require nodes and edges with different attributes. This chapter introduced the `Graph` class for undirected networks, and the `DiGraph` class for directed networks, as well as the `MultiGraph` and `MultiDiGraph` classes. In addition, this chapter demonstrated how to attach data to nodes and edges using attributes. Now you know how to access the basic properties of a network in NetworkX using these classes, but where do those networks come from? The next chapter describes various techniques for creating networks from data.

References

The following is a list of resources that you can consider to get further knowledge:

- Zachary, W. W. (1977). An information flow model for conflict and fission in small groups. Journal of anthropological research, 33(4).
- Knecht, A. B. (2008). *Friendship selection and friends' influence* (Doctoral dissertation). Utrecht University.

3
From Data to Networks

To analyze a system using NetworkX, that system must first be modeled as a network, and then be represented as an object within NetworkX. This chapter explains the basic process of creating network representations of data. The first section covers the part of the process that takes place in your head: modeling data as a network. The remaining sections demonstrate the part of the process that happens in code: creating a NetworkX Graph from data, using two different methods. In the first method, data is reformatted into one of the standard network formats supported by NetworkX. In the second method, for more complex data, a network is created from scratch, by using code to add nodes and edges one at a time.

In this chapter, we will cover the following topics:

- **Modeling data**: Giving meaning to nodes and edges
- **Network files**: Saving your networks to files
- **Networks from code**: Creating networks with code

Modeling your data

When representing data as a network, there are many decisions to make along the way. Different types of networks are helpful for understanding different types of data and for asking different types of questions. This section will take a closer look at some of the important considerations.

When creating a network from data, one of the most important questions to consider is what exactly the nodes and edges should represent. Often there are many possibilities, even for the same dataset. Any particular choice focuses on some aspects of the data, possibly discarding others. Networks are fundamentally about relationships and connections, so one way to define nodes and edges is to think about what types of relationships you're interested in. Some possibilities include the following:

- Social relationships, such as friendships, romantic relationships, or even rivalries
- Flows, such as information, people, money, fluids, or energy
- Influence, such as scientific citations, software dependencies, or protein interactions
- Connection, such as between networked computers, bones in a skeleton, neighboring countries, or railway lines
- Interaction, such as predator-prey relationships or international treaties
- Co-occurrence of words in text

Once you know what type of relationship you want to understand, the choice of nodes should be obvious: people in social networks, proteins in protein interactions, countries in international treaties, and so on. Similarly, the nature of the relationships will often suggest what type of network to use. Flows have a direction, suggesting directed networks. Rail lines allow travel in either direction, suggesting an undirected network. If you are interested in whether a very contagious disease could travel between two people, you might only need an unweighted network. But, if infection typically requires multiple exposures, you might want a weighted network to keep track of how many times two people interacted. And, of course, it is always possible to create multiple networks from the same data set in order to investigate multiple questions.

Consider, for example, Wikipedia. Wikipedia is a free online encyclopedia that allows anyone to edit any page (with some exceptions). Wikipedia is an interesting platform for several reasons. Somehow, Wikipedia has allowed millions of volunteers to work together to produce an encyclopedia that rivals professionally-edited alternatives. That level of coordination is impressive, especially if you consider how difficult it is for two people to agree on something as simple as what to eat for lunch (sometimes it takes until dinner to decide). Wikipedia is also interesting because the entire edit history of each article, as well as much of the discussion between editors is archived and publicly available, making it incredibly useful for studying large-scale collaboration.

So, what does Wikipedia look like as a network? That's a bit like asking the color of a rainbow—there's no one right answer. Let's take a look at some of the many possibilities. One type of relationship on Wikipedia is the topical relationship between articles. Articles can link to other articles when they mention related topics. For instance, the Cat article links to the Purr article. To study topical relationships, we might construct a network with nodes as articles and links as edges. And, since links take you away from one article and to another, they are best represented as directed edges. What about edge weight? At first glance, using the number of links from one article to another as an edge weight might seem to make sense. But it is conventional on Wikipedia to only link the first time a topic is mentioned, which would result in all edge weights being one. So, you could choose to use an undirected network if you care about which links exist more than how many links exist. Or you could determine edge weight by how many times a topic is mentioned, even if it is only linked once. Or, if you were interested in how links direct readers' attention, you might give higher weight to links encountered earlier in an article.

Alternatively, if you're interested in how Wikipedia editors work together, you might want to look at communication and collaboration relationships between editors. In this case, nodes are editors rather than articles. There are still many ways to define edges. One possibility is for edges to represent when one user leaves a comment on another user's talk page (typically used for one-on-one communication), which would suggest a directed edge. Alternatively, edges could represent whether two editors have worked on the same articles. Such edges could be undirected, or could use direction to represent the flow of information from earlier editors to later editors.

As the preceding example demonstrates, even a data set with a relatively simple structure can produce many different networks that are each well-suited to answering different kinds of questions. As with many things, network science is more effective (and more fun) when you use the right tool for the job. Once you've decided how to model data as a network, the data needs to be loaded into a NetworkX object, such as a `Graph`, in order to be manipulated and analyzed. Several ways to load data into NetworkX objects are described in the following sections.

Reading and writing network files

NetworkX provides support for reading and writing many network file formats. Of course, if a network has been provided in one of these formats, it will be very easy to load into NetworkX! But, even if you have data in another format, it is often possible to convert it to one of the supported formats without too much difficulty (I would guess that 90% of network science work is converting data between formats most of the rest is complaining about converting data). Spreadsheets, for instance, can often be converted to an appropriate format just by reordering columns and exporting as **tab-separated values** (TSV format). This section will describe several common formats, including adjacency list, edge list, GEXF, and JSON.

The edge list format is a simple but useful plain-text format. It supports edge attributes, but not node attributes. Edge lists are read and written with the `read_edgelist()` and `write_edgelist()` functions. Each line of an edge list network contains the IDs of two nodes, representing an edge. Here is the content of a sample edge list network, representing a fictional subway system:

```
# Example edge list network
# source target
Winegroom Uptown
Winegroom Strawshop
Uptown Strawshop
Uptown Amazelake
Strawshop Province
```

Lines starting with # are comments, and are ignored by NetworkX. By default, NetworkX will interpret any whitespace as the end of a node ID and the start of a new one. If you would like to have whitespace in a node ID, you can use the delimiter parameter to specify a different delimiter, such as the `"\t"` tab character. Before reading the network file, we store the directory containing the data in `data_dir`:

```
from pathlib import Path
data_dir = Path('.') / 'data'
```

Next, the `read_edgelist()` function creates a `Graph` class from the edge list file, like so:

```
G = nx.read_edgelist(data_dir / example.edgelist')
```

We can visualize this network as usual:

```
pos = nx.spring_layout(G)
nx.draw_networkx(G, pos)
plt.gca().margins(0.15, 0.15)
```

In addition to using `draw_networkx()` to draw the G network, we add padding to the margins to make extra room for the node labels. Putting all the preceding code together produces the following visualization:

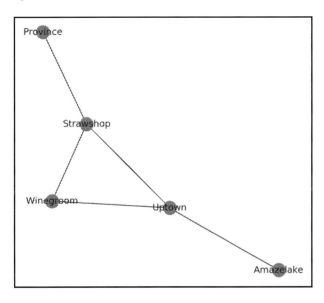

Network read from edge list file

Notice that NetworkX assumed the edge list represents an undirected network and returned a `Graph` class accordingly. If a network is directed, the `read_edgelist()` function can also return a `DiGraph` class. The only necessary change is that the `DiGraph` class must be passed as the `create_using` parameter. For directed networks, the first node on each line of the edge list will be interpreted as the source and the second as the target. The modified code for directed networks is as follows:

```
# Read edge list
G = nx.read_edgelist(
    data_dir / 'example.edgelist',
    create_using=nx.DiGraph)
# Draw network
nx.draw_networkx(G, pos)
plt.gca().margins(0.15, 0.15)
```

The preceding code should produce an output similar to this:

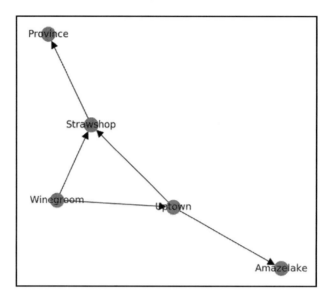

Directed network read from edge list file

The edge list format also supports weighted edges. Edge weights can be specified by adding a number as the third entry on each line of the edge list and using read_weighted_edgelist() to read the file. The weight will automatically be added to an edge attribute called weight. With these changes, the example network file now looks like this:

```
# Example edge list network
# source target weight
Winegroom Uptown 1
Winegroom Strawshop 5
Uptown Strawshop 9
Uptown Amazelake 6
Strawshop Province 3
```

The following code uses read_weighted_edgelist() to create a network with edge weights, and then draws the network with edge colors corresponding to their weight:

```
# Read edge list
G = nx.read_weighted_edgelist(
data_dir / 'weighted.edgelist')
# Extract weights
weights = [d['weight'] for s, t, d in G.edges(data=True)]
# Draw network
```

```
nx.draw_networkx(
    G, pos, width=4, edge_color=weights, edge_cmap=plt.cm.Greys)
plt.gca().margins(0.15, 0.15)
```

This code gives us a new visualization, now with weighted edges:

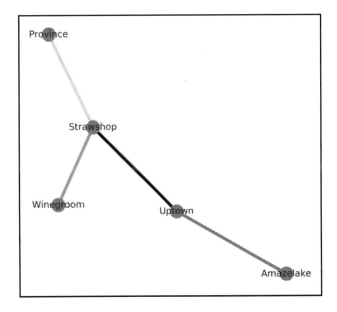

Weighted network loaded from edge list file

In addition to weights, the edge list format supports specifying additional attributes for each edge (but not for nodes). Attributes are simply appended to each line of the edge list. For example, if we want to label different routes in the example subway with colors, we can add these to the edge list like so:

```
# Example edge list network
# source target data1 data2 ...
Winegroom Uptown 1 red
Winegroom Strawshop 5 orange
Uptown Strawshop 9 blue
Uptown Amazelake 6 red
Strawshop Province 3 orange
```

These attributes can be read with either `read_edgelist()` or
`read_weighted_edgelist()` by passing the data parameter. This parameter must be a
list of 2-tuples. Each tuple is used by NetworkX to parse one of the attributes in order. The
first element of each tuple is a string that tells NetworkX which attribute to set. The second
element is an object constructor used to create edge attributes. Often these constructors are
built-in Python classes (`str`, `int`, `float`, and so on), but they can be any object constructor
that accepts a string parameter. The next example shows how to read the attributes from
the preceding edge list and draws the subway network with edges colored according to
their color attribute. Note that weight can be handled like any other attribute if you use
`read_edgelist()` rather than `read_weighted_edgelist()`:

```
# Read edge list
G = nx.read_edgelist(
    data_dir / 'attributes.edgelist',
    data=[('weight', float), ('color', str)])
# Extract colors
colors = [d['color'] for s, t, d in G.edges(data=True)]
# Draw network
nx.draw_networkx(
G, width=4, edge_color=colors)
plt.gca().margins(0.15, 0.15)
```

This code reads the color attribute of each edge and passes it to `draw_networkx()` as the
`edge_color` parameter, producing a much more colorful visualization:

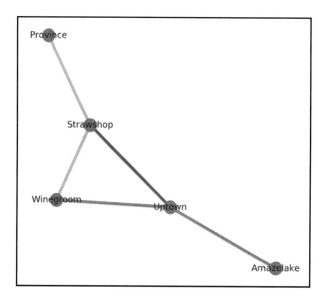

Network with attributes read from an edge list file

Sometimes attributes aren't necessary and it's convenient to have a simple, compact, plain-text representation of a network. In these cases, the adjacency list format is a good alternative to edge lists. In an adjacency list file, multiple nodes are listed on each line. NetworkX creates an edge from the first node on each line to each of the subsequent nodes on that line. As with edge lists, these edges can be directed or undirected. One of the benefits to the adjacency list format is brevity. Most edges can be specified by adding a single term, rather than two. The drawback is the inability to specify edge attributes. Sticking with the subway example, the adjacency list representation is as follows:

```
# Example adjacency list network
# source target1 target2 ...
Winegroom Uptown Strawshop
Uptown Strawshop Amazelake Winegroom
Strawshop Winegroom
Province Strawshop
```

This file can be turned into a network using the following code. No need to plot the output—it's the exact same network as before:

```
# Read adjacency list
G = nx.read_adjlist(data_dir / 'example.adjlist')
```

NetworkX also supports the export of networks in edge list and adjacency list format. The write_edgelist() and write_adjlist() functions can be used to do so. All you need to do is pass a Graph class, DiGraph class,or other NetworkX network object and specify the pathname as follows:

```
nx.write_edgelist(G, "out.edgelist") nx.write_adjlist(G, "out.adjlist")
```

Adjacency lists are convenient, and edge lists make it possible to add edge attributes, but so far none of these formats support node attributes. It's not really a party without node attributes, but luckily there are other formats that support them. These formats are a little more complex, but still possible to edit by hand in text editors if you're feeling adventurous. For the sake of demonstration, the following code adds an abbreviation attribute to each node:

```
for v in G.nodes:
    G.nodes[v]['abbreviation'] = v[0]
```

One useful format for working with node attributes is GEXF. GEXF is an XML-based format that is also used by other free/open-source network tools, such as the Gephi visualization application. The added complexity of the GEXF format makes it possible for node and edge attributes to be handled automatically by `read_gexf()` and `write_gexf()`. Exporting a network as GEXF is as simple as this:

```
import sys
nx.write_gexf(G, sys.stdout)
```

Because I have specified `sys.stdout` as the output file, the preceding code will write the output to the screen, rather than to a file. The output is given as follows for reference. I won't describe it in detail, but skimming it should give you a sense of how nodes, edges, and attributes are represented in GEXF:

```
<?xml version='1.0' encoding='utf-8'?>
<gexf version="1.2" xmlns="http://www.gexf.net/1.2draft"
xmlns:xsi="http://www.w3.org/2001/XMLSchema-instance"
xsi:schemaLocation="http://www.w3.org/2001/XMLSchema-instance">
  <graph defaultedgetype="undirected" mode="static" name="">
    <attributes class="edge" mode="static">
      <attribute id="1" title="color" type="string" />
    </attributes>
    <attributes class="node" mode="static">
      <attribute id="0" title="abbreviation" type="string" />
    </attributes>
    <meta>
      <creator>NetworkX 2.2rc1.dev_20181210023650</creator>
      <lastmodified>09/12/2018</lastmodified>
    </meta>
    <nodes>
      <node id="Winegroom" label="Winegroom">
        <attvalues>
          <attvalue for="0" value="W" />
        </attvalues>
      </node>
      <node id="Uptown" label="Uptown">
        <attvalues>
          <attvalue for="0" value="U" />
        </attvalues>
      </node>
      <node id="Strawshop" label="Strawshop">
        <attvalues>
          <attvalue for="0" value="S" />
        </attvalues>
      </node>
      <node id="Amazelake" label="Amazelake">
        <attvalues>
```

```
          <attvalue for="0" value="A" />
        </attvalues>
      </node>
      <node id="Province" label="Province">
        <attvalues>
          <attvalue for="0" value="P" />
        </attvalues>
      </node>
    </nodes>
    <edges>
      <edge id="0" source="Winegroom" target="Uptown" weight="1.0">
        <attvalues>
          <attvalue for="1" value="red" />
        </attvalues>
      </edge>
      <edge id="1" source="Winegroom" target="Strawshop" weight="5.0">
        <attvalues>
          <attvalue for="1" value="orange" />
        </attvalues>
      </edge>
      <edge id="2" source="Uptown" target="Strawshop" weight="9.0">
        <attvalues>
          <attvalue for="1" value="blue" />
        </attvalues>
      </edge>
      <edge id="3" source="Uptown" target="Amazelake" weight="6.0">
        <attvalues>
          <attvalue for="1" value="red" />
        </attvalues>
      </edge>
      <edge id="4" source="Strawshop" target="Province" weight="3.0">
        <attvalues>
          <attvalue for="1" value="orange" />
        </attvalues>
      </edge>
    </edges>
  </graph>
</gexf>
```

Finally, there are also several JSON-based formats available in NetworkX. These formats also support node attributes. In addition to being considerably more compact than GEXF, these formats are very convenient when working with JavaScript or ECMAScript, for example, when using the d3.js visualization library. One such command and the output for the example subway network are given as follows. Again, I won't describe these in detail, but you may find them useful as reference. More information is provided in the NetworkX documentation.

The following code generates a JSON representation of a network:

```
nx.node_link_data(G)
```

The resulting output is the following:

```
{'directed': False,
 'graph': {},
 'links': [{'color': 'red',
    'source': 'Winegroom',
    'target': 'Uptown',
    'weight': 1.0},
   {'color': 'orange',
    'source': 'Winegroom',
    'target': 'Strawshop',
    'weight': 5.0},
   {'color': 'blue', 'source': 'Uptown', 'target': 'Strawshop', 'weight':
9.0},
   {'color': 'red', 'source': 'Uptown', 'target': 'Amazelake', 'weight':
6.0},
   {'color': 'orange',
    'source': 'Strawshop',
    'target': 'Province',
    'weight': 3.0}],
 'multigraph': False,
 'nodes': [{'abbreviation': 'W', 'id': 'Winegroom'},
   {'abbreviation': 'U', 'id': 'Uptown'},
   {'abbreviation': 'S', 'id': 'Strawshop'},
   {'abbreviation': 'A', 'id': 'Amazelake'},
   {'abbreviation': 'P', 'id': 'Province'}]}
```

Creating a network with code

So far, you've got some handy network formats in your toolbox. But, if your data is too complex or too messy to easily convert into one of the previous formats, you might have to build your network from scratch, adding edges and nodes one at a time. Luckily, the techniques you learned in `Chapter 2`, *Working with Networks in NetworkX*, are all you really need! This section walks through a practical example of building a network programmatically from a real data set.

The example in this section is a word co-occurrence network. These networks are used to understand the relationship between words in a particular set of documents. In a co-occurrence network, nodes represent words and edge weights represent how many documents they appear in together. Here, "document could mean any collection of words: blog post, paragraph, sentence, carefully arranged dishes of alphabet soup, and so on. A warning: you might find this section a bit frightening, but only because it uses the classic Gothic horror and science fiction novel *Frankenstein; or, The Modern Prometheus* by *Mary Wollstonecraft Shelley* as the example text to construct a co-occurrence network.

The network in the following example measures word co-occurrences at the sentence level—the edge weight between words increases by one for each sentence they appear in together. The general procedure is to break the text into sentences, then break each sentence into words, and then update edges between each pair of words in the sentence. That part is relatively simple, but, as there so often is, there is also some data cleanup to be done to help the results make more sense. One of the most common steps when working with natural language data is to remove stop words such as articles and pronouns, which appear in most sentences. If you're doing advanced work in natural language processing, libraries such as NLTK provide tools to easily remove stop words. But here, I'll just create a list. For brevity, the following example only lists the first few words, but the full list is available in the sample code for this chapter:

```
# Ignore articles, pronouns, etc.
stop_words = set(['the', 'of', 'and'])
```

The following function creates a co-occurrence network from a text string. In addition to removing stop words, it removes punctuation and converts words to lowercase, so words at beginning or end of a sentence are treated the same as others. For each sentence, edges are created for each word in the sentence:

```
# This example uses regular expressions from the re package
import re
# Construct a network from a text
def co_occurrence_network(text):
    # Create a new network
    G = nx.Graph()
    # Split the text into sentences and iterate through them
    sentences = text.split('.')
    for s in sentences:
        # Remove punctuation and convert to lowercase
        clean = re.sub('[^\w\n ]+', '', s).lower()
        clean = re.sub('_+', '', clean).strip()
        # Create list of words separated by whitespace
        words = re.split('\s+', clean)
        # Create an edge for each pair of words
        for v in words:
```

```
            # Update word count, add node if necessary
            try:
                G.nodes[v]['count'] += 1
            except KeyError:
                G.add_node(v)
                G.nodes[v]['count'] = 1
            # Update edge count for each pair of words in this sentence
            for w in words:
                # Skip stop words
                if v == w or v in stop_words or w in stop_words:
                    continue
                # Skip blank space
                if len(v) == 0 or len(w) == 0:
                    continue
                # Add one to the edge's count
                try:
                    G.edges[v, w]['count'] += 1
                except KeyError:
                    # Edge doesn't exist, create it
                    G.add_edge(v, w, count=1)
    return G
```

Dividing text into chunks, as the previous function does, is called `tokenizing`. In practice, it is easier and more reliable to use a `tokenization` function from a library, such as `spaCy`, but these libraries are outside the scope of this book.

The text of Frankenstein is included with the code for this book, so, with the previous function defined, creating a co-occurrence network is simple:

```
# Read the text
with open(data_dir / 'shelley1818' / 'frankenstein.txt') as f:
    text = f.read()
# Create a network from the text
G = co_occurrence_network(text)
```

The G network now contains edges for (almost) every pair of words that co-occur in the same sentence. Sorting the edges by their count attribute reveals the most commonly co-occurring words:

```
pairs = sorted(
    G.edges(data=True),
    key=lambda e: e[2]['count'],
    reverse=True)
pairs[0:10]
[('man', 'old', {'count': 68}),
 ('country', 'native', {'count': 38}),
```

```
('first', 'now', {'count': 32}),
('death', 'life', {'count': 32}),
('human', 'being', {'count': 32}),
('natural', 'philosophy', {'count': 32}),
('eyes', 'tears', {'count': 30}),
('first', 'eyes', {'count': 28}),
('some', 'time', {'count': 28}),
('night', 'during', {'count': 28})]
```

At this point, it's tempting to visualize the network. Doing so confronts us with the following image:

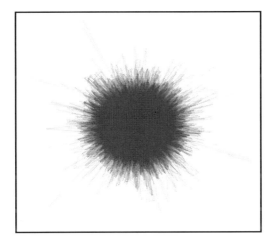

The dreaded hairball

It's not particularly easy to make sense of the preceding visualization. There are just too many nodes and edges in too small a space. Such visualizations are colloquially called **hairballs** in network science, and are generally best avoided. However, with a little creativity, it's still possible to produce some more helpful visualizations. Doing so often involves focusing on a particular aspect of the network, or a particular set of nodes. For example, it is how frequently two characters in *Frankenstein* are mentioned in the same sentence using the following code:

```
# Count co-occurrences for characters only
characters = [
    'creature', 'monster', 'victor', 'elizabeth',
    'william', 'henry', 'justine']
G_focus = G.subgraph(characters)
# Create list of edge counts
counts = [G_focus.edges[e]['count'] for e in G_focus.edges]
```

```
# Create spring layout
pos = nx.spring_layout(G_focus)

# Create figure and draw nodes
plt.figure()
nx.draw_networkx_nodes(G_focus, pos)
# Draw edges
nx.draw_networkx_edges(
    G_focus, pos, width=8,
    edge_color=counts, edge_cmap=plt.cm.Blues, alpha=0.5)
nx.draw_networkx_edges(G_focus, pos, edge_color="#7f7f7f",alpha=0.5)
# Draw labels
nx.draw_networkx_labels(G_focus, pos)
plt.tight_layout()
```

The subgraph() method of Graph creates a new graph containing a subset of the nodes in the original, as well as any edges between those nodes. Visualizing the resulting subgraph produces the following:

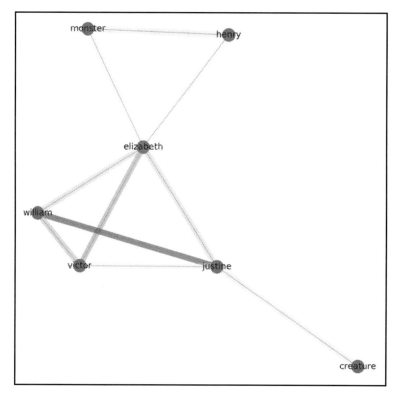

Co-occurrence of characters in *Frankenstein*

The preceding example keeps only the nodes representing character names and the edges between them. Edge colors are based on the count edge attribute. Now, it's much easier to find meaningful information in the visualization. For example, the creature and the monster refer to the same character, but different terms are used depending on which other characters are mentioned. Some more advanced visualization techniques will be covered in Chapter 11, *Visualization*.

Summary

This chapter has demonstrated the process of getting data into NetworkX for analysis. This chapter discussed the types of questions that are important to consider when creating a network from data, and applied them to the example of Wikipedia. This chapter also gave examples of loading networks from standard formats and building networks from scratch. The next chapter introduces affiliation networks—those with two types of nodes.

References

The following is a list of resources that you can consider to get further knowledge:

- Shelley, Mary Wollstonecraft. (1818). *Frankenstein; or The Modern Prometheus*. Urbana, Illinois: Project Gutenberg. Retrieved February 21, 2016, from www.gutenberg.org/ebooks/19033.

4
Affiliation Networks

Edges represent connections or relationships between two nodes and only those two nodes, but some relationships involve more than two nodes. Typically, such relationships take the form of multiple nodes belonging to a common group or sharing a common affiliation. This relationship structure can be set up by adding a second type of node representing the groups or affiliations. Such networks are called **affiliation networks**. This chapter describes how to work with complex relational data using affiliation networks, as well as how affiliation networks are represented and manipulated in NetworkX.

The topics that are covered in this chapter include the following:

- **Nodes and affiliations**: How data with complex relationships can be represented by affiliation networks and how to recognize an affiliation network structures
- **Affiliation networks in NetworkX**: How to create, detect, manipulate, and visualize affiliation networks using NetworkX
- **Projections**: How to convert affiliation networks into networks with a single type of node

Nodes and affiliations

In the game **Six Degrees of Kevin Bacon**, perhaps the most widely-known application of network science principles, the goal is to find a link between a given actor and the actor Kevin Bacon. For example, Jon Hamm can be connected to Kevin Bacon as follows: Jon Hamm was in *Bridesmaids* with Rose Byrne, who was in *X-Men: First Class*, with Kevin Bacon. This game takes place on a network. In one version of the network, nodes represent actors and edges represent movies that two actors both appeared in. This version of the network (let's call it the **actor-actor** network) is sufficient for finding Kevin Bacon, but it doesn't fully represent the relationships between actors and movies. Movies typically have a cast of many actors, but each edge in the actor-actor network only corresponds to two actors. Consequently, there need to be many edges for each movie. On the other hand, if a movie had only a single actor, there would be no corresponding edges and it wouldn't appear in the actor-actor network at all! It would be much more convenient if there was also a node for each movie. In this modified network (let's call it the **actor-movie** network), there are two types of nodes, movies and actors, and each edge connects one movie to one actor in that movie. Such networks are called affiliation networks because the edges often represent affiliations between people (like actors) and groups of people (like a movie cast).

Formally, an affiliation network (or bipartite network, if you're feeling mathematical) is one that has two types of nodes and only allows edges from one type of node to other. This is in contrast to standard **single-mode** networks, which have only one type of node. The two types of node are sometimes called **top** and **bottom**, or **left** and **right**, but those are just ways to distinguish between the two types and don't have any special meaning. Really, you could call the two types of nodes whatever you like (such as widdershins and deiseil, or dalek and kaled).

Affiliation networks are useful for representing many-to-many relationships. For example, a movie can contain many actors, and an actor can appear in many movies; or a postal code can cover many cities, and a city can contain many postal codes. While most network science usually focuses on single-mode networks, there are often affiliation networks hiding behind them! In fact, the only systems that can't be represented by an affiliation network are those for which relationships or connections always involve precisely two nodes.

Here are some examples of common systems that can be represented by affiliation networks:

Data type	Node	Affiliation
Email	Sender/recipient	Message
Coauthorship	Author	Publication
Corporate directorate	Board member	Corporate board
Legislation	Representative	Bill
Book translations	Language	Book
Media coverage	Nation/topic	Media outlet
Online hashtags	Hashtag	Post
Natural language	Word	Document
Cover songs	Musician	Song
Metabolic networks	Chemical	Reaction
Cuisine	Ingredient	Recipe

When representing affiliation networks visually, the two types of node are usually distinguished using different shapes and/or colors. An example network is shown in following *figure*. Often, circles and squares are used, but here I have used circles and hexagons (hexagons are cool!). In this case, the circles represent musicians and the hexagons represent songs recorded by that musician (be they original compositions or covers). Musicians are connected only to songs and songs are connected only to musicians:

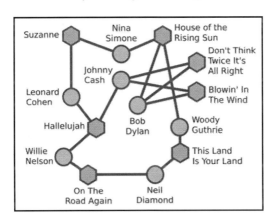

Affiliation network of musicians and songs

Affiliation networks in NetworkX

Affiliation networks are represented in NetworkX using the same classes as other networks: `Graph` and `DiGraph`. The only difference is that you need to keep track of which nodes are of which type. In NetworkX, this is done by using a container (`list`, `set`, and so on) to store all node IDs for one node type. For convenience, the node type can also be stored as a node attribute. A network can be tested for an affiliation network structure using the `sets()` function. Usually, this function can also find the nodes of each type (the exception being when the network has groups of nodes that are not connected to the rest of the network). The following example loads our dear old friend from Chapter 2, *Working with Networks in NetworkX*, the Zachary karate club network, and checks it for affiliation network structure:

```
# Import bipartite module
from networkx.algorithms import bipartite
from networkx import NetworkXError
# Load Zachary karate network
G = nx.karate_club_graph()
try:
    # Find and print node sets
    left, right = bipartite.sets(G)
    print("Left nodes\n", left)
    print("\nRight nodes\n", right)
except NetworkXError as e:
    # Not an affiliation network
    print(e)
Graph is not bipartite.
```

It looks like the karate club network is not an affiliation network. Really, that is no surprise. There's really no reason it should be—anyone can be friends with anyone else. However, for the sake of demonstrating a point, it is possible to turn it into an affiliation network. But what is the second type of node? Friends are affiliated with each other by their friendships, so the friendships—or edges—can be used as the second type of node. The following code creates edges connecting two types of node: one representing the original node, and the other representing the old edges. The nodes themselves are added automatically by NetworkX. Note that when working with affiliation networks, the network objects are often named `B` for bipartite or biadjacency (or maybe for Bacon):

```
B = nx.Graph()
B.add_edges_from([(v, (v, w)) for v, w in G.edges])
B.add_edges_from([(w, (v, w)) for v, w in G.edges])
try:
    # Find and print node sets
    left, right = bipartite.sets(B)
```

```
    print("Left nodes\n", left)
    print("\nRight nodes\n", right)
except NetworkXError as e:
    # Not an affiliation network
    print(e)
```
Left nodes
```
{0, 1, 2, 3, 5, 6, 7, 8, 9, 10, 11, 12, 13, 14, 15, 16, 17, 18, 19, 20,
21, 22, 23, 24, 25, 26, 27, 28, 29, 30, 31, 32, 33}
```

Right nodes
```
{(5, 6), (15, 32), (0, 7), (14, 33), (23, 32), (0, 3), (22, 33), (31, 32),
(24, 31), (32, 33), (1, 2), (30, 33), (0, 21), (2, 9), (26, 29), (24, 27),
(0, 17), (0, 11), (2, 13), (2, 27), (28, 31), (26, 33), (8, 33), (0, 5),
(2, 3), (0, 1), (2, 7), (3, 12), (5, 10), (5, 16), (0, 19), (0, 13), (20,
33), (29, 32), (24, 25), (28, 33), (0, 31), (1, 30), (18, 33)}
```

This time, NetworkX finds two sets of nodes. Looking more closely, one set contains only node IDs, while the other contains only edges, which means that NetworkX has correctly identified the affiliation structure created by the code. If we only wanted to know whether the network was an affiliation network, rather than finding the node sets, we could simply use the is_bipartite() function, as shown in the following code:

```
bipartite.is_bipartite(B)
```
True

Before going into more advanced examples of affiliation networks, it's necessary for us to have an important discussion about the birds and the bees. The remainder of this section will use pollinator networks—the relationships between animal species and the plants they help pollinate—as an example (what did you think I meant?). This specific example comes from a study of some species in *Cap de Creus, Catalonia* (Bartomeus et al., 2008). The data is provided in TSV format and could be easily converted to edgelist format (as discussed in Chapter 3, *From Data to Networks*), but the following code shows how to parse it directly from the raw TSV. This example also uses the connected_components() function (discussed in Chapter 7, *In-Between: Communities*) to ignore nodes that are not connected to the rest of the network:

```
# Create data directory path
from pathlib import Path
data_dir = Path('.') / 'data'
B = nx.Graph()
with open(data_dir / 'bartomeus2008' / 'Bartomeus_Ntw_nceas.txt') as f:
    # Skip header row
    next(f)
    for row in f:
        # Break row into cells
        cells = row.strip().split('\t')
```

```
            # Get plant species and pollinator species
            plant = cells[4].replace('_', '\n')
            pollinator = cells[8].replace('_', '\n')
            B.add_edge(pollinator, plant)
            # Set node types
            B.nodes[pollinator]["bipartite"] = 0
            B.nodes[plant]["bipartite"] = 1
    # Only consider connected species
    B = B.subgraph(list(nx.connected_components(B))[0])
```

We could use `sets()` to find the node sets again, but there's an easier way. When the preceding `Graph` was built, a `bipartite` attribute was created to track which node set each node belongs to: 0 for pollinators and 1 for plants. The following code creates lists for each node set:

```
# Get node sets
pollinators = [v for v in B.nodes if B.nodes[v]["bipartite"] == 0]
plants = [v for v in B.nodes if B.nodes[v]["bipartite"] == 1]
```

With lists for each node set, it is now possible to draw the pollinator network in NetworkX. The following code uses all of the usual visualization functions, but draws the nodes in two steps—one for each node set:

```
# Create figure
plt.figure(figsize=(30,30))
# Calculate layout
pos = nx.spring_layout(B, k=0.9)
# Draw using different shapes and colors for plant/pollinators
nx.draw_networkx_edges(B, pos, width=3, alpha=0.2)
nx.draw_networkx_nodes(B, pos, nodelist=plants, node_color="#bfbf7f",
node_shape="h", node_size=3000)
nx.draw_networkx_nodes(B, pos, nodelist=pollinators, node_color="#9f9fff",
node_size=3000)
nx.draw_networkx_labels(B, pos)
```

This code draws pollinators as orange hexagons and plants as blue circles, producing the following visualization:

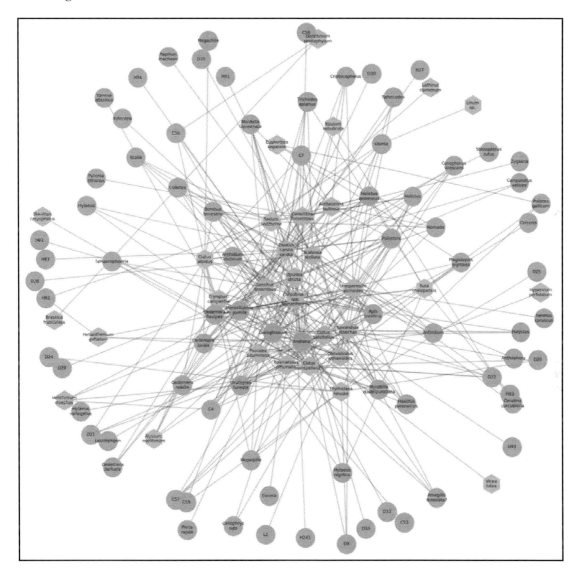

Plant-pollinator network

Projections

While affiliation networks are useful for representing the full structure of many-to-many relationships, it is sometimes easier to work with standard single-mode networks. This might be the case if an analysis focuses on a particular type of node, or if a necessary technique is only available for single-mode networks, or if the affiliation network has too many nodes to visualize clearly. Luckily, it is possible to create single-mode networks out of an affiliation network using a process called **projection**. And, as you might expect, NetworkX makes it easy.

Single-mode networks built from affiliation networks are called **co-affiliation** networks, because the nodes are connected by an edge if they have common affiliations. There are several types of projections that are used to create co-affiliation networks, but they all revolve around the same idea: connecting nodes with a common neighbor in the original affiliation network. The simplest possible projection is an unweighted projection, which creates an unweighted edge between nodes with one or more common neighbors. The following code uses the `projected_graph()` function to project the pollinator network onto the plant nodes and plots the resulting co-affiliation network:

```
# Create co-affiliation network
G = bipartite.projected_graph(B, plants)
# Create figure
plt.figure(figsize=(24,24))
# Calculate layout
pos = nx.spring_layout(G, k=0.5)
# Draw edges, nodes, and labels
nx.draw_networkx_edges(G, pos, width=3, alpha=0.2)
nx.draw_networkx_nodes(G, pos, node_color="#bfbf7f", node_shape="h",
node_size=10000)
nx.draw_networkx_labels(G, pos)
```

Running this code produces the following visualization of the connections between the plants:

Plant-plant co-affiliation network

Note how densely connected the core of the network is. This occurs because each neighbor of a pollinator becomes connected to all of that pollinator's other neighbors, creating a group of plants that are all connected to each other, a structure known as a clique. This highly connected core is a common characteristic of co-affiliation networks.

It is also possible to project the pollinator network onto the pollinators instead of the plants. The following code does just that, and plots the resulting co-affiliation network:

```
# Create co-affiliation network
G = bipartite.projected_graph(B, pollinators)
# Create figure
```

```
plt.figure(figsize=(30,30))
# Calculate layout
pos = nx.spring_layout(G, k=0.5)
# Draw edges, nodes, and labels
nx.draw_networkx_edges(G, pos, width=3, alpha=0.2)
nx.draw_networkx_nodes(G, pos, node_color="#9f9fff", node_size=6000)
nx.draw_networkx_labels(G, pos)
```

This code is almost exactly the same as the previous example, with the only difference being that it projects onto `pollinators` instead of `plants`. As a result, it produces the following visualization of the pollinators:

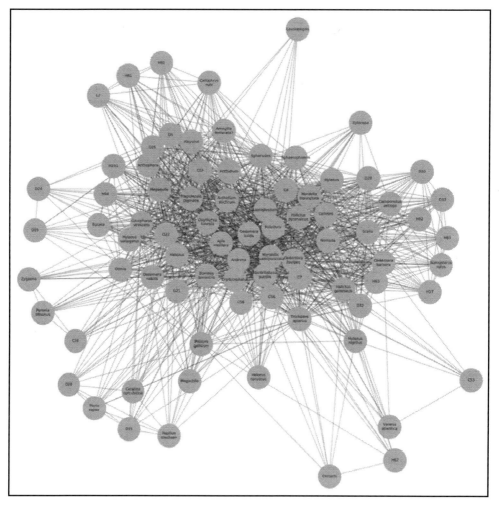

Pollinator-pollinator co-affiliation network

Just as with the plant-plant co-affiliation network, the pollinator-pollinator network has a densely connected core. There is a pleasing symmetry between the plant-plant and pollinator-pollinator networks: plants connected by pollinators in one and pollinators connected by plants in the other.

In the preceding unweighted projections, considerable information is lost concerning the structure of the affiliation network. An edge might mean that two nodes have one common affiliation or one hundred. One way to capture some of this information is to use a weighted projection. Weighted projections turn a weighted or unweighted affiliation network into a weighted co-affiliation network. Some of the structural information lost is recaptured in the edge weights. One common way to calculate edge weights is by simply counting the number of common neighbors. This technique can be interpreted as counting the number of paths between two nodes in the original affiliation network. In NetworkX, this projection is achieved using the `weighted_projected_graph()` function, shown in the following code snippet. The computed weight is stored in the `weight` edge attribute:

```
G = bipartite.weighted_projected_graph(B, plants)
list(G.edges(data=True))[0]
```

('Urospermum\npicrioides', 'Alyssum\nmaritimum', {'weight': 4})

Alternatively, edge weights can be calculated using a similarity measure, such as the Jaccard index. The Jaccard index for two nodes is the number of common neighbors divided by the number of nodes that neighbor either of the nodes, and ranges from 0 (no common neighbors) to 1 (all neighbors are in common). The `overlap_weighted_projection_graph()` function creates a projection using the Jaccard index. The following code calculates such a projection for the pollinator network and visualizes edge weights using a color gradient:

```
# Create co-affiliation network
G = bipartite.overlap_weighted_projected_graph(B, pollinators)
# Get weights
weight = [G.edges[e]['weight'] for e in G.edges]
# Create figure
plt.figure(figsize=(30,30))
# Calculate layout
pos = nx.spring_layout(G, weight='weight', k=0.5)
# Draw edges, nodes, and labels
nx.draw_networkx_edges(G, pos, edge_color=weight, edge_cmap=plt.cm.Blues,
width=6, alpha=0.5)
nx.draw_networkx_nodes(G, pos, node_color="#9f9fff", node_size=6000)
nx.draw_networkx_labels(G, pos)
```

The preceding code uses the `edge_color` parameter of `draw_networkx_edges()` to color edges based on their projected weight, allowing the strength of the connections to be visualized:

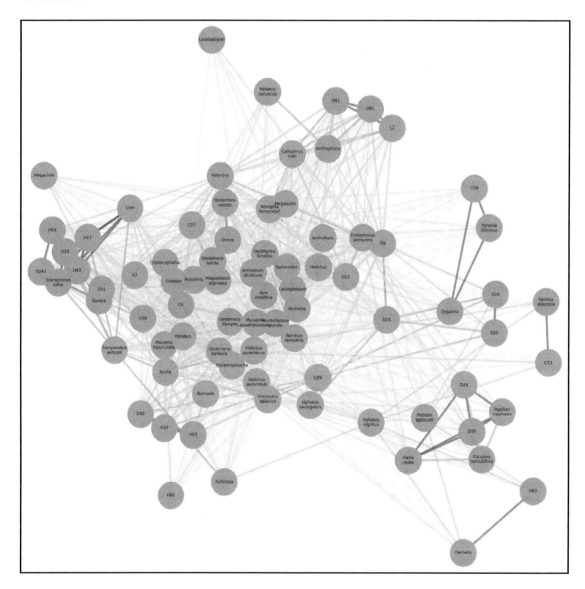

Weighted projection of plant-pollinator affiliation networks

This diagram uncovers some additional information about the pollinator-pollinator network. While most nodes have many neighbors, the weight of those edges is relatively low. However, some nodes have fewer but stronger connections, showing isolated groups of pollinators that have much in common with each other. Ultimately, the type of projection to use depends on the nature of the network data and the question you hope to answer.

Summary

This chapter introduced affiliation networks and the tools provided by NetworkX for working with affiliation networks, with special attention to using projections to create co-affiliation networks. Affiliation networks are ubiquitous in network data. Whenever there is a symmetrical relationship that can connect more than two things, there is an underlying affiliation structure. Many single-mode networks are really co-affiliation networks—projections of affiliation networks onto one type of node. Different projections have different interpretations, such as the number of paths or similarities. Choosing an appropriate projection for the data and for the question being asked can reveal important properties of a network that might otherwise be overlooked. Even as you encounter standard single-mode networks in the rest of this book, and in real-world data, it is often helpful to consider what type of affiliation networks might be hiding behind them, and what can be learned from them. The next part of this book describes techniques for understanding the structure of networks at various scales. The following chapter begins this discussion by introducing ways to measure small-scale network structures.

References

The following is a list of resources that you can consider to get further knowledge:

- Bartomeus, I., Vilà, M., & Santamaría, L. (2008). Contrasting effects of invasive plants in plant–pollinator networks. *Oecologia*, 155(4).

5
The Small Scale - Nodes and Centrality

Network science can be used to understand systems not just in terms of which parts are connected, but also in terms of how their neighbors and their neighbor's neighbors. In other words, network science can be used to understand the structure of a networked system are connected. The following three chapters describe how network science is used to understand network structure at various scales. This chapter focuses on the **small-scale**, or **micro-scale**, structure. The micro-scale structure describes the positions and roles played by specific nodes within the greater network. Such analysis can be used to identify influential individuals, bottlenecks in flows, and convenient locations for assembling information or resources. These properties (and others) can be characterized using centrality measures, which quantify various structural properties of individual nodes. This chapter describes several important centrality measures and demonstrates how to use NetworkX to calculate and interpret them.

The topics in this chapter include the following:

- **Centrality**: Quantifying a node's structural properties using centrality measures
- **Betweenness centrality**: Identifying nodes that act like bridges using betweenness centrality
- **Eigenvector centrality**: Identifying highly-connected nodes using eigenvector centrality
- **Closeness centrality**: Quantifying the distance between a node and the rest of the network using closeness centrality
- **Local clustering**: Quantifying the interconnectedness of a node's neighborhood

Centrality – finding key nodes

My interest in network science was, in part, inspired by my experience with hackerspaces and makerspaces. These spaces are member-run organizations that provide space and tools for do-it-yourself/technology/art projects. In 2009, I worked with several others in the Detroit area to start a space called i3 Detroit. During my time at i3 Detroit, I was struck by the creativity and innovation happening in i3 Detroit and other spaces, not just in the projects that were being created, but also in the unique types of volunteer-run, non-hierarchical organizations that were being developed. One of the keys to this innovation was the way ideas were spread within and between spaces. Ideas were spread from space to space by participants in national events and by members who went on hackerspace tours. Ideas were spread within spaces by the regulars who seemed to know everyone and who were happy to share their knowledge and experience. Some volunteer administrators kept in touch with those from other spaces and regularly discussed ideas on mailing lists or in person, allowing an idea in one space to very quickly spread to others if the idea seemed like a good one. The rapid development and spread of the hackerspace model relied on individuals who could spread information and ideas in different ways because of the types of relationships they had—in other words—due to their position in the social network structure.

 The current generation of hackerspaces in North America started after attendees of the 2007 Chaos Communication Camp, inspired by European hackerspaces, returned to the US to start Noisebridge (in San Francisco), NYC Resistor (in Brooklyn), and HacDC (in Washington, D.C.). These spaces served as models for others, and, over the next few years, hackerspaces popped up in most major US cities. They can also be great places to meet others interested in network science and free software!

Whether nodes represent people, places, computers, or atoms, the location of a node within a network's structure is closely related to the role it plays in the overall system. Different structures enable different roles. So, by quantifying the structural properties of a node, it is possible to understand the role played by that node. Numerical measures that characterize the network properties of a node are called **centrality** measures. Centrality is often introduced as a measure of importance, but there are many ways in which a node can be important. For example, one of the simplest centrality measures is **degree centrality**. A node's degree centrality is just the number of neighbors it has (in a directed network, there is both in-degree and out-degree). In a social network, degree centrality is a measure of popularity, and might be a good way to guess who throws the best parties [but who wants to go to parties when you can do network science?]. Degree centrality is a pretty rudimentary example, but the following sections present more sophisticated measures that are often used in network science. Each centrality measure quantifies a different type of importance and can be helpful in answering different types of questions.

Bridges, brokers, and bottlenecks – betweenness centrality

In the popular children's game **Telephone**, one player starts by whispering a message to another, who then whispers that message to another, and so on. At the end, the last player recites the message out loud. Typically, the final message bears no resemblance to the original. So, a message that began as "follow the funky flow" might end up as "if every pork chop were perfect, we wouldn't have hotdogs". Every time a message passes from person to person, it has the possibility of changing, possibly because it was misheard, or possibly because it was deliberately changed. In more complex social networks, such as organizations and social movements, the individuals who connect different parts of the network have the greatest ability to filter, amplify, and alter information. Such individuals are called **brokers**, while edges that span distant parts of a network are called **bridges**. The importance of such nodes and edges isn't limited to social networks. In flow networks—such as railroads, water pipes, and telecommunications systems—nodes connecting distant parts of a network can act as bottlenecks, limiting the amount of flow. Identifying such bottlenecks makes it possible to increase their capacity and protect them from failures and attacks. Bridges and brokers are important because they stand between different parts of a network. Accordingly, the type of centrality used to identify bridges and brokers is called **betweenness centrality**.

To understand betweenness centrality, it is first necessary to understand the concept of a shortest path. A path is a sequence of nodes, moving along edges from neighbor to neighbor (in a directed network, paths follow out-edges). Paths can also be assigned a length, which is helpful for determining whether any two nodes are near or far from each other. In an unweighted network, the path length is typically the number of edges in a path, sometimes called the number of "hops" if you prefer a more rabbit-based definition. In a weighted network, there are many ways to calculate path length depending on the scenario. If edge weights represent distance or travel time, it makes sense to calculate path length by simply adding the weights of all the edges in the path. The path length can then be used to define the distance between two nodes: the length of the shortest path connecting them. The following diagram shows two paths of different lengths connecting nodes **A** and **B**. The path on the right happens to be the shortest path connecting them. Since that path is of length **2**, the distance between **A** and **B** in the pictured network is **2**:

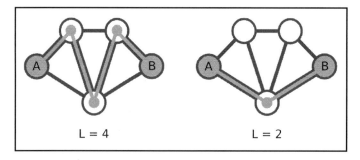

Two possible paths between nodes A and B

Betweenness centrality is based on the assumption that the greater the number of shortest paths pass through a node (or edge), the more it acts as a broker (or bridge). To calculate betweenness centrality, the shortest paths between each pair of nodes are found. The betweenness centrality value for a node or edge is just the number of these paths that pass through it. There are a couple of caveats. First, by convention, paths are not considered to pass through their endpoints and do not contribute to their betweenness centrality. Also, you might wonder what happens if there are two shortest paths of the same length. In this case, each path contributes 1/2 to the betweenness centrality of its nodes/edges (or 1/3 if there are 3 paths, and so on).

The following diagram shows an example network and the calculated betweenness values for each node and edge. The shortest path for each pair of nodes (excluding trivial paths of length 1) are shown. The node betweenness is the sum of paths that pass through that node. The edge betweenness is the number of nontrivial paths that pass through that edge, plus 1 for the edge itself:

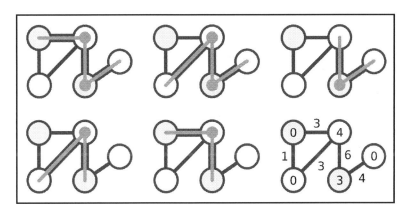

All non-trivial shortest paths in an example network and the resulting betweenness centralities

Betweenness centrality is easily calculated in NetworkX using the `betweenness_centrality()` function. This function returns a `dict` that maps node IDs to centrality values. If the `normalized` parameter is `True` (the default), betweenness values are divided by the number of node pairs, which can be helpful for comparing betweenness values across networks of different sizes. If the `endpoints` parameter is set to `True` (`False` by default), then path endpoints will be included in the centrality calculation.

The example in this chapter is a covert network, namely that of British suffragettes in the early 20th century. Covert networks occur in systems where membership is meant to be secret, as might be the case when members fear retaliation from an oppressive regime. These networks are particularly interesting to study because there is a tension between the need for secrecy and the need to spread information throughout the network. The following example comes from the arrest records of British suffragettes (Edwards & Crossley, 2009). These records form an affiliation network (aren't you glad you read `Chapter 4`, *Affiliation Networks*?) between individuals and mass arrest events.

The following code loads the data, constructs an affiliation network, and projects it into a co-affiliation network containing only person nodes:

```python
# Create empty affiliation network and list of people
B = nx.Graph()
people = set()
# Load data file into network
from pathlib import Path
data_dir = Path('.') / 'data'
with open(data_dir / 'edwards2009' / '50_ALL_2M.csv') as f:
    # Parse header
    events = next(f).strip().split(",")[1:]
    # Parse rows
    for row in f:
        parts = row.strip().split(",")
        person = parts[0]
        people.add(person)
        for j, value in enumerate(parts[1:]):
            if value != "0":
                B.add_edge(person, events[j], weight=int(value))
# Project into person-person co-affiliation network
from networkx import bipartite
G = bipartite.projected_graph(B, people)
```

With the network loaded into NetworkX, the following code calculates the betweenness centrality and shows the 10 individuals with the highest value:

```python
betweenness = nx.betweenness_centrality(G, normalized=False)
sorted(betweenness.items(), key=lambda x:x[1], reverse=True)[0:10]

[('Maud Joachim', 52896.533246052524),
 ('Ada Wright', 26344.263264276862),
 ('Patricia Woodlock', 24774.923422322467),
 ('Emily Duval', 19517.906214119495),
 ('Mary Leigh', 19404.22583377209),
 ('Mabel Capper', 18221.362811581737),
 ('Sylvia Pankhurst', 18127.59688636897),
 ('Elsie Evans', 15674.806298703466),
 ('Winifred Mayo', 15600.989680321372),
 ('Vera Wentworth', 13233.504078942538)]
```

High betweenness centralities suggest that these individuals were important information brokers in the suffragette movement, and indeed, they were all notable suffragettes. The following diagram shows a 1910 photograph of Maud Joachim, taken by Colonel Linley Blathwayt at Eagle House, a famous refuge for suffragettes. Of course, network analysis alone can't reveal why these individuals were important. That requires incorporating richer data and methods (Edwards, 2014). However, looking at other network measures can still help to shed some light on the role these individuals played in the suffragette movement:

Maud Joachim (right) and William Blathwayt planting a tree at Eagle House in 1910

Hubs – eigenvector centrality

Imagine having an important message that needs to reach an entire group (for example, your employer or school), but only being able to give that message to one person. Who would you tell? You'd want to find someone well-connected to the entire network. You might try the person with the highest degree centrality (the most friends). The downside to that approach is that their friends might not be well connected to the rest of the network. In a hypothetical company, for example, the Director of East Coast Sales might know the most people, but might not know how to reach anyone in other departments or regions. Instead, it would be better to find someone who is highly connected to other highly-connected people, such as the CEO (or, more likely, their assistant). Such individuals are sometimes called **hubs**, because, like the center of a spoked wheel, they interconnect many different points. This concept of highly-connected hubs is captured well by a measure called **eigenvector centrality**.

You're probably wondering what exactly an eigenvector is. Don't worry! I won't try to explain it here. Instead, here's an illustrative example. Imagine sending a message to a social network as follows: you write a few million copies of the message on pieces of paper, and then give those individual pieces of paper to a random person in the network [hopefully after doing some stretches for your overworked wrists]. Those people then take each piece of paper they have and give it randomly to one of their neighbors (following out-edges if the network is directed). This final step is repeated several times. In most networks, this process will eventually result in a situation where each person receives as many pieces of paper as they give away [trust me, I'm a mathematician]. After that point, the number of pieces of paper each person has will not change. The more well-connected an individual is, the more pieces of paper they will end up with. The eigenvector centrality is closely related to this number. The more well-connected a node, the higher the eigenvector centrality.

In NetworkX, the `eigenvector_centrality()` function can be used to calculate eigenvector centrality. As with other centrality measures, this function returns a `dict` that maps node IDs to centrality values. The following example applies this function to the suffragette network and prints the top 10 hubs in the network:

```
eigenvector = nx.eigenvector_centrality(G)
sorted(eigenvector.items(), key=lambda x:x[1], reverse=True)[0:10]

[('Maud Joachim', 0.11587964174472963),
 ('Caroline A Downing', 0.11437066100686191),
 ('Kitty Marion', 0.11344996012448627),
 ('Mabel Capper', 0.10991776240126284),
 ('Annie Bell', 0.10834705221110298),
 ('Grace Chappelow', 0.10818185244249957),
 ('Winifred Mayo', 0.10803831965810341),
 ('Ellen Pitfield', 0.10518714292397996),
 ('Dorothy Agnes Bowker', 0.1049391922254588),
 ('Mrs Maud Fussell', 0.10490326319130663)]
```

Just as before, these are all notable activists from the suffragette movement. Some of these individuals also appeared in the previous section, including the most central, Maud Joachim. However, some of the individuals with high eigenvector centrality don't have particularly high betweenness centrality, such as Caroline A. Downing. Individuals with high eigenvector centrality create many short paths between others, but not necessarily the shortest paths.

Closeness centrality

The measure known as **closeness centrality** is one of the oldest centrality measures used in network science, proposed by the sociologist, Alex Bavelas, in 1950. Closeness is defined as the reciprocal of **farness**. What is farness? It's the reciprocal of closeness, of course! More helpfully, the farness of a node is the sum of distances between that node and all other nodes. So, a node with high closeness centrality is literally close to other nodes. Nodes with high closeness have, on average, short paths to many other nodes, which can be helpful for disseminating resources quickly.

The following example uses the NetworkX `closeness_centrality()` function to calculate the closeness centrality values for the suffragette network and display the top 10:

```
closeness = nx.closeness_centrality(G)
sorted(closeness.items(), key=lambda x:x[1], reverse=True)[0:10]

[('Maud Joachim', 0.5357241748956739),
 ('Winifred Mayo', 0.5009438937877011),
 ('Caroline A Downing', 0.5009438937877011),
 ('Mabel Capper', 0.5006919099377073),
 ('Kitty Marion', 0.49793672684150186),
 ('Ada Wright', 0.4898501559823633),
 ('Patricia Woodlock', 0.4886477746471095),
 ('Vera Wentworth', 0.48769011119851163),
 ('Evelyn Whurry', 0.4874512815652116),
 ('Annie Bell', 0.4869743233640714)]
```

Nearly everyone in this list appears in at least one of the other top 10 lists, but only Maud Joachim, Winifred Mayo, and Mabel Capper appear in all three. Once again, Maud Joachim comes out on top, clearly an important figure in the suffragette movement, despite not being less well-known than some other suffragettes who didn't make these lists. It is perhaps an important lesson that the important structural roles played by brokers and hubs in a network are easily and often obscured.

Local clustering

The last structural measure presented in this chapter is a little different from the ones seen so far. Betweenness, eigenvector, and closeness centrality all characterize a node by its relation to other nodes in the network. The measure presented in this section concerns the relationships between a node's neighbors, rather than those of the node itself. It is often useful to consider whether a node's neighbors tend to be connected to each other. In a social network, this question translates to asking whether the friend of a friend is also your friend, a property known as **transitivity** [to mathematicians who enjoy polysyllabic words]. The result of such relationships are triangles: three nodes, all mutually connected. The tendency for such triangles to arise is called clustering. When strong clustering is present, it often suggests robustness, and redundancy in a network—if one edge disappears, a path still exists via the other two. Clustering is measured via the **local clustering coefficient**, defined as the fraction of all pairs of a node's neighbors that have an edge between them.

In NetworkX, the number of triangles between a node and its neighbors can be calculated using the `triangles()` function. The local clustering coefficient can be found using the `clustering()` function. The following example finds the nodes with the most triangles:

```
triangles = nx.triangles(G)
sorted(triangles.items(), key=lambda x:x[1], reverse=True)[0:10]

[('Maud Joachim', 19687),
 ('Caroline A Downing', 18201),
 ('Kitty Marion', 17696),
 ('Mabel Capper', 16811),
 ('Winifred Mayo', 16455),
 ('Annie Bell', 16065),
 ('Grace Chappelow', 16018),
 ('Ellen Pitfield', 14910),
 ('Mrs Maud Fussell', 14841),
 ('Dorothy Agnes Bowker', 14750)]
```

Now, we can use `clustering()` to find the local clustering coefficient for these nodes:

```
clustering = nx.clustering(G)
[(x, clustering[x]) for x in sorted(people, key=lambda x:eigenvector[x],
reverse=True)[0:10]]

[('Maud Joachim', 0.23595330552759),
 ('Caroline A Downing', 0.34999903851700864),
 ('Kitty Marion', 0.3670988486671507),
 ('Mabel Capper', 0.33992518451117176),
 ('Annie Bell', 0.4233201581027668),
 ('Grace Chappelow', 0.43461037551551984),
```

```
('Winifred Mayo', 0.3480477177545582),
('Ellen Pitfield', 0.4828993392926545),
('Dorothy Agnes Bowker', 0.5058125578683859),
('Mrs Maud Fussell', 0.5006071645415908)]
```

Unsurprisingly, Maud Joachim shows up as having the highest centrality in terms of triangles. More surprisingly, these top nodes have local clustering coefficients in roughly the 25%-50% range, while the nodes in the network span the entire 0%—100% range. The three individuals common to the top 10 lists for all centrality measures have local clustering coefficients ranging from 24%-35%. If an individual's local clustering coefficient is low, it suggests they aren't well-connected. If the coefficient is high, it suggests that an individual's connections are redundant. So, the most central individuals have high absolute numbers of triangles, but midrange local clustering coefficients.

Summary

This chapter has shown how to analyze the microscale structure of networks by calculating centrality measures and other node-based measures of network structure. Betweenness centrality identifies bridges and brokers: edges and nodes that connect otherwise poorly connected parts of a network. Eigenvector centrality identifies nodes that are connected to other well-connected nodes. Closeness centrality identifies nodes that are, on average, closest to other nodes. Finally, the triangle count and local clustering coefficient quantify how well-connected a node's friends are. By examining a historical social network of suffragette activists, we saw that ranking highly on one centrality value doesn't necessarily mean a node ranks highly on others. While sometimes correlated, different centrality values measure different things, so meaningful results require choosing a measure well-suited to the question at hand. The following chapter steps back to look at ways of understanding the large-scale structure of a network.

References

The following is a list of resources that you can consider to get further knowledge:

- Edwards, G., & Crossley, N. (2009). Measures and meanings: Exploring the ego-net of Helen Kirkpatrick Watts, militant suffragette. Methodological Innovations Online, 4(1).
- Edwards, G. (2014). Infectious innovations? The diffusion of tactical innovation in social movement networks, the case of suffragette militancy. Social Movement Studies, 13(1).

6

The Big Picture - Describing Networks

Large-scale structures can vary widely from network to network. These differences are often indicative of different types of networks (for example, social versus technological). Large-scale structures can also have important implications for functional properties, such as resilience to errors and attack. This chapter describes a variety of structural measures used to classify entire networks. Examples are given for a selection of real-world networks from different types of systems.

Topics covered in this chapter include the following:

- **Global structure**: Understanding the properties of whole networks
- **Diameter and shortest paths**: How to measure the size of a network
- **Global clustering**: Using clustering to quantify interconnections between neighbors of neighbors
- **Resilience**: How properties such as density and minimum cut can quantify error and attack tolerance
- **Inequality**: Learning to measure the equality or inequality in network structures

The global structure of networks

When trying to understand the general trends in a network, or exploring the differences between networks, staring at hairballs is not particularly useful (as much as my cat tries to convince me otherwise). Quantitative measures of large-scale network structures make it possible to characterize and compare different networks.

Large-scale structures can help you approach questions including the following:

- Is a network becoming more or less resilient to failures as it grows?
- How far does data or electricity need to travel as it moves across a network?
- How centralized is a network?
- Do nodes cluster into tightly connected groups?

Datasets

This chapter explores large-scale network structures using a variety of example networks. The first of these is the familiar karate club network (Zachary, 1977) introduced in Chapter 2, *Working with Networks in NetworkX*. This network is representative of social networks. As usual, the karate club network can be loaded directly from NetworkX:

```
G_karate = nx.karate_club_graph()
mr_hi = 0
john_a = 33
```

The second example used in this chapter is the German electrical grid (Mureddu, 2016). Nodes in this network represent electrical generators and transformers. Edges represent high-voltage lines used to transport electricity. Because each node in this network corresponds to a physical space, most connections are located between geographically nearby nodes. This local structure is common across infrastructure networks. The following code loads the network from an edge list formatted file:

```
# Load Germany electrical grid
with open(data_dir / 'mureddu2016' / '0.2' / 'branches.csv', 'rb') as f:
    # Skip header
    next(f)
    # Read edgelist format
    G_electric = nx.read_edgelist(
        f,
        delimiter="\t",
        create_using=nx.Graph,
        data=[('X', float), ('Pmax', float)])
```

The third and final example is a telecommunication network. Specifically, the example is the European GÉANT network. GÉANT connects research and educational networks across Europe. The nodes in this network correspond to points of presence, while the edges correspond to high-capacity telecommunication links. The following code loads the network from a GraphML formatted file:

```
G_internet = nx.read_graphml(data_dir / 'UAITZ' / 'Geant2012.graphml')
```

A **point of presence (PoP)** is a location where internet service providers connect routers and servers to their high-capacity telecommunication links. At these points, internet traffic is routed within and between different networks.

The following code visualizes the three example networks:

```
# Create a figure
plt.figure(figsize=(7.5, 2.75))
# Plot networks
plt.subplot(1, 3, 1);
plt.title("Karate")
nx.draw_networkx(G_karate, node_size=0, with_labels=False)
plt.subplot(1, 3, 2)
plt.title("Electric")
nx.draw_networkx(G_electric, node_size=0, with_labels=False)
plt.subplot(1, 3, 3)
plt.title("Internet")
nx.draw_networkx(G_internet, node_size=0, with_labels=False)
# Adjust layout
plt.tight_layout()
```

Running the preceding code visualizes (from left to right) the karate, electrical grid, and internet PoP networks:

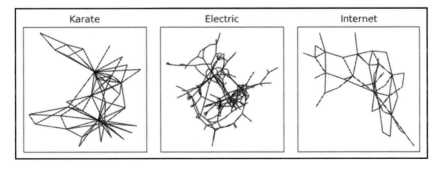

Three real-world networks

Diameter and mean shortest path

The size of a network can be quantified in several ways. In Chapter 5, *The Small Scale – Nodes and Centrality*, the distance between two nodes was defined as the length of the shortest path between them. With a way to measure distance, it becomes possible to define size based on that distance.

NetworkX provides several convenient functions for finding distances and shortest paths. The shortest paths between two particular nodes can be found using the all_shortest_paths() function:

```
list(nx.all_shortest_paths(G_karate, mr_hi, john_a))
[[0, 8, 33], [0, 13, 33], [0, 19, 33], [0, 31, 33]]
```

If you only need to know the distance, the shortest_path_length() function will provide that:

```
nx.shortest_path_length(G_karate, mr_hi, john_a)
2
```

On the other hand, the distance between all node pairs can be found using the shortest_path_length() function. This function produces an iterator that can be turned into a dict of dict objects, with the keys of the first corresponding to source node IDs, and the keys of the second corresponding to target node IDs. The following example finds all distances in the karate club network and uses the resulting dict object to find the distance between John A. and Mr. Hi:

```
length_source_target = dict(nx.shortest_path_length(G_karate))
length_source_target[0][33]
```

Networks can be characterized according to their distribution of shortest path lengths. The following function draws a histogram of all shortest path lengths within a network:

```
def path_length_histogram(G, title=None):
    # Find path lengths
    length_source_target = dict(nx.shortest_path_length(G))
    # Convert dict of dicts to flat list
    all_shortest = sum([
        list(length_target.values())
        for length_target
        in length_source_target.values()],
    [])
    # Calculate integer bins
    high = max(all_shortest)
    bins = [-0.5 + i for i in range(high + 2)]
    # Plot histogram
```

```
plt.hist(all_shortest, bins=bins, rwidth=0.8)
plt.title(title)
plt.xlabel("Distance")
plt.ylabel("Count")
```

Now, let's compare the path length distributions of the three example networks:

```
# Create figure
plt.figure(figsize=(7.5, 2.5))
# Plot path length histograms
plt.subplot(1, 3, 1)
path_length_histogram(G_karate, title="Karate")
plt.subplot(1, 3, 2)
path_length_histogram(G_electric, title="Electric")
plt.subplot(1, 3, 3)
path_length_histogram(G_internet, title="Internet")
# Adjust layout
plt.tight_layout()
```

The preceding code uses `path_length_histogram()` to visualize the distribution of shortest path lengths in the three example networks:

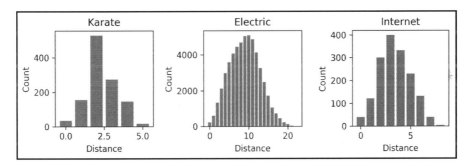

Distributions of shortest path lengths in real-world networks

The karate club and internet networks both have very small path lengths, while the electrical network has much larger lengths. Social networks tend to have short paths, known as the small world phenomenon. Infrastructure networks such as the electrical grid have longer paths because high voltage lines are costly, and are only used to connect nearby points. While the internet network is also infrastructural, it is composed of interconnected long-distance links that help information move quickly across long distances. These redundant long-distance links result in smaller path lengths than other infrastructure networks.

While informative, the full path length distributions are a bit unwieldy, so it is helpful to use summary measures. One such measure is the mean shortest path length, also known as the *characteristic length*, which can be calculated as follows:

```
nx.average_shortest_path_length(G_karate)
2.408199643493761
```

 In a disconnected network, where the network can be divided into two or more components with no edge between them, the mean path length becomes infinite. This difficulty can be resolved in several ways, such as using a harmonic rather than arithmetic mean, or by averaging the mean shortest path lengths within each connected component. Which method is appropriate depends on the type of network being analyzed.

The mean shortest path lengths for the other two networks are given by the following command:

```
nx.average_shortest_path_length(G_electric)
9.044193487671748
```

```
nx.average_shortest_path_length(G_internet)
3.528205128205128
```

Alternatively, the size of a network can, instead, be characterized by the largest path length—called the **diameter**. The diameters of the three example networks can be found using the `diameter()` function:

```
nx.diameter(G_karate)
5
```

```
nx.diameter(G_karate)
22
```

```
nx.diameter(G_karate)
8
```

The preceding results are larger than the mean shortest path lengths, but give a similar overall picture of the relative sizes of the networks.

Unlike the mean shortest path length, the diameter only depends on a single path. As a result, a single outlier can greatly increase the diameter. However, it can be a good measure of the worst case path length.

Global clustering

The level of clustering or transitivity in a network can be quantified using triangles, just as the transitivity was quantified for individual nodes in Chapter 5, *The Small Scale – Nodes and Centrality*. These measures describe, overall, how common triangles are within a network.

The simplest measure of large-scale clustering is **transitivity**: the fraction of possible triangles that are present. The following example uses the transitivity() function to calculate this value for the example networks:

```
nx.transitivity(G_karate)
0.2556818181818182

nx.transitivity(G_electric)
0.07190412782956059

nx.transitivity(G_internet)
0.135678391959799
```

An alternative approach is to average the local clustering coefficient (described in Chapter 5, *The Small Scale – Nodes and Centrality*) over all nodes. This measure is sometimes called the global clustering coefficient. In NetworkX, it is calculated using the average_clustering() function, as in the following example:

```
nx.average_clustering(G_karate)
0.5706384782076823

nx.average_clustering(G_karate)
0.06963512677798392

nx.average_clustering(G_karate)
0.1544047619047619
```

Measuring resilience

Resilience is the ability of a system to withstand errors and attacks. In an electrical grid, for example, resilience would mean keeping power flowing when a transmission line or generator broke down. In traffic, it could mean the ability to reroute cars when a street is closed due to an accident.

Resilience is fundamentally a network property because it is usually achieved with redundant paths. When one path is no longer available, the others can still be used.

The simplest (and crudest) measure of resilience is the **density** of a network: the fraction of possible edges that exist. The more edges present in a network, the more redundant paths exist between its nodes. The following code uses the `density()` function to calculate this value for the example networks:

```
nx.density(G_karate)
0.13903743315508021

nx.density(G_karate)
0.011368341803124411

nx.density(G_karate)
0.0782051282051282
```

A network is generally considered sparse if the number of edges is close to N (the number of nodes), and dense if the number of edges is close to N^2.

Minimum cuts

More sophisticated measures of resilience are based on the concept of minimum cuts. A **minimum cut** or **min-cut** is the number of nodes (or edges) that need to be removed to separate the network into two unconnected parts. Minimum cuts can be found either between two specific nodes, or over all pairs of nodes.

In NetworkX, the minimum cut between two nodes is found using the `minimum_st_node_cut()` function. Note that this function is in the `connectivity` package and needs to be imported separately in addition to the base `networkx` package. The following code finds the minimum node cut between Mr. Hi and John A. in the karate club network:

```
import networkx.algorithms.connectivity as nxcon
nxcon.minimum_st_node_cut(G_karate, mr_hi, john_a)
{2, 8, 13, 19, 30, 31}
```

The preceding means that the 2, 8, 12, 19, 30, 31 nodes need to be removed in order to separate the network into disconnected halves, with one containing Mr. Hi, and the other containing John A.

Similarly, the minimum edge cut can be established as follows:

```
nxcon.minimum_st_edge_cut(G_karate, mr_hi, john_a)
 {(0, 8),
 (0, 31),
 (1, 30),
 (2, 8),
 (2, 27),
 (2, 28),
 (2, 32),
 (9, 33),
 (13, 33),
 (19, 33)}
```

If you only need to know the size of the minimum cut, you can use the node_connectivity() or edge_connectivity() functions in the base networkx package. The following example calculates these values for the karate club network:

```
nx.node_connectivity(G_karate, mr_hi, john_a)
6
```

```
nx.edge_connectivity(G_karate, mr_hi, john_a)
10
```

Connectivity

Minimum cuts can be used to define connectivity measures for entire networks. These measures are very useful for quantifying the resilience of a network.

The node connectivity is the smallest min-cut over all node pairs. The edge connectivity is defined similarly. The actual node and edge cuts can be found using the connection package:

```
nxcon.minimum_node_cut(G_karate)
{0}
```

```
nxcon.minimum_edge_cut(G_karate)
{(11, 0)}
```

The connectivity can be calculated using the `node_connectivity()` and `edge_connectivity()` functions without specifying source and target nodes. The following example finds the node connectivity for the three example networks:

```
nx.node_connectivity(G_karate)
1
```

```
nx.node_connectivity(G_electric)
1
```

```
nx.node_connectivity(G_internet)
1
```

It seems that all of these networks can be divided into disconnected parts by the removal of a single node! The next time your power goes out, you can blame the low connectivity of the electrical grid.

The preceding connectivity measure finds the size of the smallest min-cut, but removing that won't affect all the paths in the network. After that node or edge has been removed, the network will be divided, but within each half, nodes are still connected to each other.

A better measure of reliability can be found by averaging the connectivity over all nodes or edges using the `average_node_connectivity()` and `average_edge_connectivity()` functions. Note that these values can take a long time to calculate, even for small networks. The following code calculates the average node connectivity of the example networks:

```
nx.average_node_connectivity(G_karate)
2.2174688057040997
```

```
nx.average_node_connectivity(G_electric)
1.5188029361942406
```

```
nx.average_node_connectivity(G_internet)
1.7346153846153847
```

Centralization and inequality

Networks can also be classified by how **centralized** they are—how much of their centrality is concentrated in one or a few nodes. Unequal distributions are more centralized. As an example, the most centralized network would be all nodes connected to a single hub node.

The following code plots histograms of the eigenvector centralities for each of the example networks:

```
# Function to plot a single histogram
def centrality_histogram(x, title=None):
    plt.hist(x, density=True)
    plt.title(title)
    plt.xlabel("Centrality")
    plt.ylabel("Density")

# Create a figure
plt.figure(figsize=(7.5, 2.5))
# Calculate centralities for each example and plot
plt.subplot(1, 3, 1)
centrality_histogram(
    nx.eigenvector_centrality(G_karate).values(), title="Karate")
plt.subplot(1, 3, 2)
centrality_histogram(
    nx.eigenvector_centrality(G_electric, max_iter=1000).values(),
title="Electric")
plt.subplot(1, 3, 3)
centrality_histogram(
    nx.eigenvector_centrality(G_internet).values(), title="Internet")

# Adjust the layout
plt.tight_layout()
```

The preceding code defines the `centrality_histogram()` function to plot node centralities, and applies it to the three example networks, producing the following output:

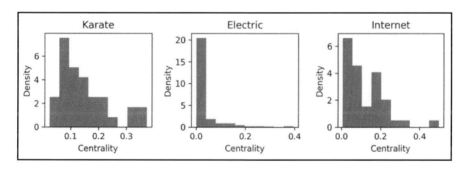

Distributions of eigenvector centrality in real-world networks

Different measures of node centrality (discussed in `Chapter 5`, *The Small Scale – Nodes and Centrality*) give rise to different measures of network centralization. There are also many ways to combine node centralities into a single measure of centralization.

One way to measure the inequality of a set of values is called the **entropy** (or, more specifically, the Shannon entropy). The meaning of entropy is beyond the scope of this book, but it is enough to know that the more unevenly distributed a set of numbers is, the higher its entropy. The following function will return the entropy of a list of numbers:

```
import math
def entropy(x):
    # Normalize
    total = sum(x)
    x = [xi / total for xi in x]
    H = sum([-xi * math.log2(xi) for xi in x])
    return H
```

If you have the `scipy` package installed, you can easily calculate entropy using `scipy.stats.entropy()`.

The Shannon entropy was first described by Claude Shannon, the mathematician who developed a theoretical framework now known as information theory. He also rode a unicycle and developed a mathematical theory of juggling.

Calculating the entropy of eigenvector centralities in each of the example networks gives the following:

```
entropy(nx.eigenvector_centrality(G_karate).values())
```
4.842401948329853

```
entropy(nx.eigenvector_centrality(G_electric, max_iter=1000).values())
```
6.030447144924192

```
entropy(nx.eigenvector_centrality(G_internet).values())
```
4.86203726163741

We see that the electrical grid is notably more centralized than the other two networks. Electricity is typically generated at a small number of generators, and then sent to substations, followed by consumers. This highly centralized architecture is captured well by the eigenvalue centrality and entropy.

Other measures of inequality are sometimes used to analyze distributions of node attributes. The Gini index is particularly popular in economics. It ranges from 0 to 1, with 1 being the highest level of inequality. The Gini index can be calculated with the following function:

```
def gini(x):
    x = [xi for xi in x]
    n = len(x)
    gini_num = sum([sum([abs(x_i - x_j) for x_j in x]) for x_i in x])
    gini_den = 2.0 * n * sum(x)
    return gini_num / gini_den
```

Applying the Gini index to the example networks gives similar results to those found using entropy:

```
gini(nx.eigenvector_centrality(G_karate).values())
0.3244949051532847

gini(nx.eigenvector_centrality(G_electric, max_iter=1000).values())
0.787950636595495

gini(nx.eigenvector_centrality(G_internet).values())
0.43432860097262216
```

Summary

This chapter has described many different techniques for quantifying the large-scale structure of networks. Network size can be quantified using the diameter or mean shortest path. Global clustering can be used to quantify how likely a node's neighbors are to be neighbors with each other. Connectivity measures, such as the minimum or average node/edge connectivity, are calculated by finding minimum cuts, and quantify network resilience. The chapter concluded by showing how inequality measures such as entropy and the Gini index can be used to turn small-scale centrality measures into large-scale measures of network centralization. The next chapter discusses medium-scale network structures and community detection.

References

The following is a list of resources that you can consider to get further knowledge:

- Mureddu, M. (2016). Representation of the German transmission grid for Renewable Energy Sources impact analysis. arXiv preprint arXiv:1612.05532.

7
In-Between - Communities

Larger than individual nodes, but smaller than entire networks, the medium-scale or **meso-scale** structure of a network characterizes groups of nodes—called **communities**—and their interrelations. NetworkX provides many tools for analyzing community structure. This chapter uses data from an online social network to demonstrate medium-scale network analysis with NetworkX.

Topics in this chapter include the following:

- **Communities**: How nodes cluster into densely connected groups
- **Community detection**: How to identify communities of nodes and partition networks
- **Cliques**: How to understand networks by finding the most highly-connected components
- **K-Cores**: How to simplify networks by focusing on the most highly-connected nodes

Communities – networks within networks

When the TCP/IP suite of telecommunication protocols was introduced in 1974, it suddenly became possible for computer networks using different hardware and software to communicate with one another—to internetwork—creating what we now know as the internet. On a related note, many of the approximately 13,000 proteins found in fruit flies interact with at least one other protein. Among these, smaller groups can be found in which each protein interacts with most of the others. It may not be immediately obvious what fruit flies have to do with the internet (aside from both being found on apples). The connection is this: as with many different kinds of networks, both the internet and protein interaction networks have smaller sub-networks with both internal structure and external relationships. In network science, these groups of highly interrelated nodes are called communities.

In computer science, communities are sometimes called **clusters**, and community detection is referred to as **clustering**. In network science, however, the measure of connection transitivity is called clustering. Interdisciplinary work can often feel like a comedy of errors.

Community structure can have important consequences for networked systems. In social networks, ideas often spread easily within communities, but have a difficult time crossing to other communities. On the other hand, a contagious disease might spread across a community just as easily.

Communities can also represent nodes with functional similarities. The accounting department of a company might form a community. Proteins related to cell mitosis might form a community. And internet routers operated by the same internet service provider almost certainly form a community. Community structure can be used to infer possible functional similarities.

It can also be informative to analyze the relationships between different communities; for example, individuals that speak the same language form a community. In this example, bilingual individuals interconnect different communities. The strength or number of connections between communities might shed light on how similar two languages are, or how culturally or geographically close the language speakers are.

The rich insights that can be gained from analyzing community structure make it a staple of network science.

Community detection in NetworkX

NetworkX provides several community detection algorithms. There are many ways to define communities, and many ways to search for them. However, in general, the NetworkX community detection functions take a `Graph` object and return a `list` or iterator over communities, represented as a `set` of node IDs.

The simplest type of community detection searches for non-overlapping communities. In other words, a network is partitioned into communities such that each node belongs to exactly one community.

Modularity maximization

One approach to finding such a partition is to define a function that quantifies the quality of a set of partitions, and then adjust the partition to maximize the quality. One popular quality measure is called **modularity**. The mathematical definition of modularity is discussed in Appendix A, but the general idea is that edges within communities should be more common than edges across communities.

Finding the maximum modularity partition is computationally difficult, but luckily, some very good approximation methods exist. The NetworkX `greedy_modularity_communities()` function implements Clauset-Newman-Moore community detection. Each node begins as its own community. The two communities that most increase the modularity are then merged (known as a **greedy** strategy). This is repeated until merging any further would decrease the modularity. The preceding example uses Clauset-Newman-Moore community detection to find communities in the Zachary karate club network (Zachary, 1977):

```
# Generate the network
G_karate = nx.karate_club_graph()
# Find the communities
communities = sorted(nxcom.greedy_modularity_communities(G_karate),
key=len, reverse=True)
# Count the communities
len(communities)
3
```

We see that `greedy_modularity_communities()` finds three communities. Now, let's visualize them to see what they represent.

Visualizing

In order to visualize communities, it will be necessary to define some helper functions. First, it is convenient to set a property on nodes and edges to specify their community. The following helper functions do exactly this:

```
def set_node_community(G, communities):
    '''Add community to node attributes'''
    for c, v_c in enumerate(communities):
        for v in v_c:
            # Add 1 to save 0 for external edges
            G.nodes[v]['community'] = c + 1

def set_edge_community(G):
    '''Find internal edges and add their community to their attributes'''
```

```
        for v, w, in G.edges:
            if G.nodes[v]['community'] == G.nodes[w]['community']:
                # Internal edge, mark with community
                G.edges[v, w]['community'] = G.nodes[v]['community']
            else:
                # External edge, mark as 0
                G.edges[v, w]['community'] = 0
```

The usual convention is to visualize communities using color. Features such as texture can also be used. The following function maps the integers 1 to 16 to unique colors:

```
def get_color(i, r_off=1, g_off=1, b_off=1):
    r0, g0, b0 = 0, 0, 0
    n = 16
    low, high = 0.1, 0.9
    span = high - low
    r = low + span * (((i + r_off) * 3) % n) / (n - 1)
    g = low + span * (((i + g_off) * 5) % n) / (n - 1)
    b = low + span * (((i + b_off) * 7) % n) / (n - 1)
    return (r, g, b)
```

Now that these helper functions have been defined, the following code can be used to annotate nodes and edges with their communities, and find the corresponding colors:

```
# Set node and edge communities
set_node_community(G_karate, communities)
set_edge_community(G_karate)

# Set community color for nodes
node_color = [
    get_color(G_karate.nodes[v]['community'])
    for v in G_karate.nodes]

# Set community color for internal edges
external = [
    (v, w) for v, w in G_karate.edges
    if G_karate.edges[v, w]['community'] == 0]
internal = [
    (v, w) for v, w in G_karate.edges
    if G_karate.edges[v, w]['community'] > 0]
internal_color = [
    get_color(G_karate.edges[e]['community'])
    for e in internal]
```

Now, let's take a look at the network using this additional data! The following code visualizes the karate club network, with each community drawn in a different color:

```
karate_pos = nx.spring_layout(G_karate)
# Draw external edges
nx.draw_networkx(
    G_karate, pos=karate_pos, node_size=0,
    edgelist=external, edge_color="#333333")
# Draw nodes and internal edges
nx.draw_networkx(
    G_karate, pos=karate_pos, node_color=node_color,
    edgelist=internal, edge_color=internal_color)
```

The first call to `draw_networkx()` draws only the external edges, while the second draws internal edges and nodes, producing the following diagram:

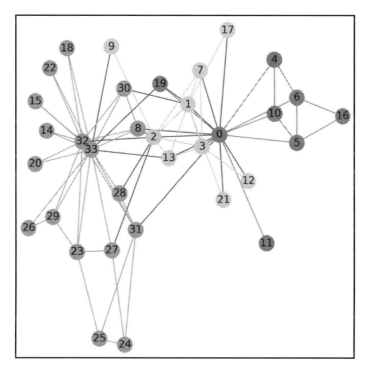

Clauset-Newman-Moore communities in the Zachary karate network

In the resulting visualization, one community is centered around Mr. Hi (node ID 0), one is centered around John A. (node ID 33), and the third is composed of nodes between the other two communities.

An online social network

The same community detection algorithm can be used on much larger networks, such as online social networks. The following example uses a social network constructed from combining the online social networks of 10 individuals (McAuley & Leskovec, 2012). The following code loads and visualizes the network:

```
# Load data file into network
from pathlib import Path
data_dir = Path('.') / 'data'
G_social = nx.read_edgelist(
    data_dir / 'mcauley2012' / 'facebook_combined.txt')

# Calculate layout and draw
pos = nx.spring_layout(G_social, k=0.1)
nx.draw_networkx(
    G_social, pos=pos, node_size=0,
    edge_color="#333333", alpha=0.05, with_labels=False)
```

Using a spring layout and drawing only edges, the preceding code produces the following visualization:

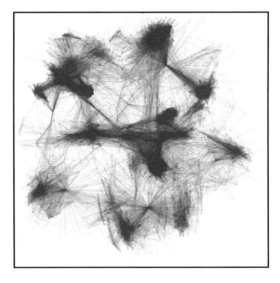

An online social network

Looking at the visualization, there appears to be a high level of community structure. The preceding example uses `greedy_modularity_communities()` to find those communities:

```
communities = sorted(nxcom.greedy_modularity_communities(G_social),
key=len, reverse=True)
len(communities)
13
```

As with the karate club network previously, we can visualize the communities using color. First, the `community` property of each node and each internal edge is set:

```
set_node_community(G_social, communities)
set_edge_community(G_social)
```

Next, we create lists containing the external and internal edges:

```
external = [
    (v, w) for v, w in G_social.edges
    if G_social.edges[v, w]['community'] == 0]
internal = [
    (v, w) for v, w in G_social.edges
    if G_social.edges[v, w]['community'] > 0]
```

We then use our `get_color()` helper function to create a list of colors for the internal edges:

```
internal_color = [
    get_color(G_social.edges[e]['community'])
    for e in internal]
```

Finally, the following code uses `draw_networkx()` to visualize the network:

```
# Draw external edges
nx.draw_networkx(
    G_social, pos=pos, node_size=0,
    edgelist=external, edge_color="#333333",
    alpha=0.2, with_labels=False)
# Draw internal edges
nx.draw_networkx(
    G_social, pos=pos, node_size=0,
    edgelist=internal, edge_color=internal_color,
    alpha=0.05, with_labels=False)
```

The first call to `draw_networkx()` draws the external edges in gray, while the second draws internal edges in a color corresponding to their community:

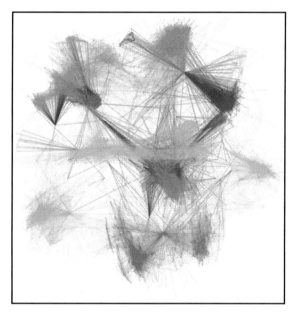

Communities in an online social network

Girvan-Newman – betweenness-based communities

The preceding examples used the modularity-based Clauset-Newman-Moore method for finding communities, which is only one of many existing community detection algorithms. NetworkX supports several others, which may be more appropriate in some cases. For example, the Girvan-Newman algorithm works by first assigning all nodes to a single large community and repeatedly splitting it into smaller communities.

In particular, the Girvan-Newman method is based on betweenness centrality (discussed in Chapter 5, *The Small Scale – Nodes and Centrality*). Betweenness centralities are first assigned to edges, and then the most central edges are removed until one of the communities is divided into two. This procedure repeats until each node is in its own community. The process can be stopped at any point in order to produce a specific number of communities, or a quality measure such as modularity can be used to estimate a good stopping point.

The Girvan-Newman method needs to recalculate betweenness at each step, making it computationally demanding. When working with very large networks in particular, other algorithms may be necessary.

In NetworkX, Girvan-Newman community detection is implemented by the `girvan_newman()` function in the community module. It returns an iterator of partitions, with each element further subdividing the previous one. For example, applying `girvan_newman()` to the Zachary karate club network returns an iterator, with the first element containing two communities:

```
result = nxcom.girvan_newman(G_karate)
communities = next(result)
len(communities)
2
```

As before, we annotate each node and internal edge with its community:

```
# Set node and edge communities
set_node_community(G_karate, communities)
set_edge_community(G_karate)
```

We then use the communities to generate node color:

```
# Set community color for nodes
node_color = [
    get_color(G_karate.nodes[v]['community'])
    for v in G_karate.nodes]
```

We then identify the internal and external edges, and assign a color to internal ones:

```
# Set community color for internal edges
external = [
    (v, w) for v, w in G_karate.edges
    if G_karate.edges[v, w]['community'] == 0]
internal = [
    (v, w) for v, w in G_karate.edges
    if G_karate.edges[v, w]['community'] > 0]
internal_color = [
    get_color(G_karate.edges[e]['community'])
    for e in internal]
```

Using the community information established previously, the following code visualizes the karate network and the communities found using `girvan_newman()`:

```
# Draw external edges
nx.draw_networkx(
    G_karate, pos=karate_pos, node_size=0,
    edgelist=external, edge_color="#333333", with_labels=False)
# Draw nodes and internal edges
nx.draw_networkx(
    G_karate, pos=karate_pos, node_color=node_color,
    edgelist=internal, edge_color=internal_color)
```

The final visualization has two communities, connected by gray external edges:

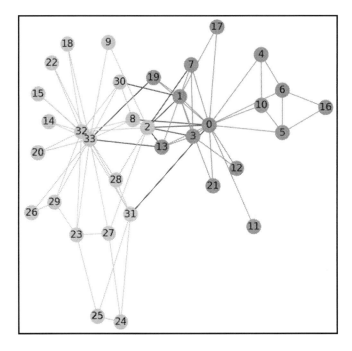

Girvan-Newman communities in the Zachary karate club network.

If, instead, we want to find a certain number of communities, for instance, four, we can use the `itertools islice()` function to pick a certain element out of the iterator returned by `girvan_newman()`. The following example shows how to do this:

```
import itertools
result = nxcom.girvan_newman(G_karate)
communities = next(itertools.islice(result, 2, 3))
```

The remainder of the visualization code is exactly the same as before and omitted here. Using the third element returned by `girvan_newman()` produces the following visualization:

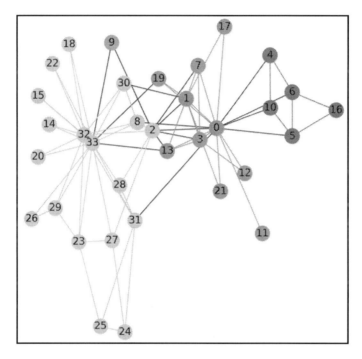

Third iteration of Girvan-Newman community detection

The communities found previously have each been divided into two different communities. Subsequent values taken from the iterator will subdivide these even further.

Cliques

In the densest neighborhoods of a network, it is sometimes possible to find groups of nodes that are all connected to each other. Such groups are called **cliques**. Identification of cliques is another way to analyze the medium-scale structure of a network. Because cliques are highly interconnected, the nodes in a clique rarely belong to different communities. In fact, cliques often form the cores of communities.

Chapter 4, *Affiliation Networks*, described how to transform an affiliation network into a single-mode network using projections. For each node removed by such projections, its neighbors are connected into a clique. Cliques can give clues to an underlying affiliation network structure.

NetworkX provides the `find_cliques()` function to find cliques in a network. This function returns an iterator over all cliques in an arbitrary order. For example, using this function on the karate club network gives the following:

```
cliques = list(nx.find_cliques(G_karate))
cliques
[[0, 1, 17],
 [0, 1, 2, 3, 13],
 ...
 [25, 23]]
```

The largest of these cliques, called the *maximal clique,* is the densest part of the network. It can be found and visualized as follows:

```
# Find max clique
max_clique = max(cliques, key=len)
max_clique
[0, 1, 2, 3, 13]

# Visualize maximum clique
node_color = [(0.5, 0.5, 0.5) for v in G_karate.nodes()]
for i, v in enumerate(G_karate.nodes()):
    if v in max_clique:
        node_color[i] = (0.5, 0.5, 0.9)
nx.draw_networkx(G_karate, node_color=node_color, pos=karate_pos)
```

The preceding code first initializes all node colors to gray, and then sets the color to blue for nodes in the maximal clique:

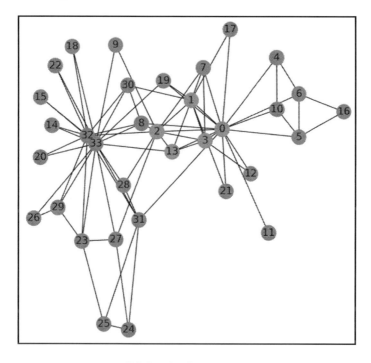

Nodes in maximal clique. colored blue

While finding cliques can be helpful for identifying the nodes that form the core of a network, it is computationally difficult (NP hard, as computer scientists say). For very small networks, such as the karate club, NetworkX works well to find cliques. For larger networks, cliques may not be a practical tool for analyzing structure. Luckily, other methods exist.

K-cores

In the previous section, we saw that cliques often form the cores of networks and communities, but that they are computationally difficult to find. In larger networks, k-cores can be a practical alternative for finding dense regions. A **k-core** is created by removing all nodes of degree less than k from a network. The number k can be anything you choose. The larger k is, the more nodes will be stripped away.

The nodes that remain in a k-core are highly connected to their neighbors. However, different parts of the network might become disconnected from each other after low-degree nodes are removed. The result is that a k-core consists of islands of highly connected nodes. These islands form the core of the network (hence the name k-core). Any remaining connections can be interpreted as highly-connected backbones that join different parts of the network.

NetworkX provides the `k_core()` function to find k-cores. This function can be run quickly, even for relatively large networks. The preceding example finds the 30-core (blue) and the 60-core (orange) of the social network introduced earlier in the chapter:

```
# Find k-cores
G_core_30 = nx.k_core(G_social, 30)
G_core_60 = nx.k_core(G_social, 60)

# Visualize network and k-cores
nx.draw_networkx(
    G_social, pos=pos, node_size=0,
    edge_color="#333333", alpha=0.05, with_labels=False)
nx.draw_networkx(
    G_core_30, pos=pos, node_size=0,
    edge_color="#7F7FEF", alpha=0.05, with_labels=False)
nx.draw_networkx(
    G_core_60, pos=pos, node_size=0,
    edge_color="#AFAF33", alpha=0.05, with_labels=False)
```

This code draws the network three times: first, in its entirety (gray), then including just the 30-core (blue), and then including just the 60-core (orange):

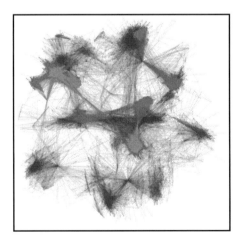

30-core and 60-core in an online social network

Note that the larger communities are all centered around blue 30-cores, while only a few communities contain nodes from the 60-core. Those communities remaining in the 60-core are the most densely connected, suggesting they may play an important role in the network. Similarly, the nodes and edges of the 60-core that lay between different communities are likely to be important brokers and bridges.

Summary

Some of the most interesting structure in networks takes place not at the smallest or largest scales, but in-between. Groups of nodes and interrelations between those groups can reveal underlying affiliations, hint at functional similarities between nodes, and identify channels likely to spread contagions of diseases or ideas.

This chapter demonstrated how to find communities in NetworkX using Clauset-Newman-Moore modularity-based communities, as well as Girvan-Newman betweenness-based communities. The chapter also introduced cliques and k-cores, and showed how to use them to identify densely connected regions of a network. Communities, cliques, and k-cores provide the basic tools necessary to analyze the medium-scale structure of networks. The next chapter focuses specifically on social networks and their unique properties.

References

The following is a list of resources that you can consider to get further knowledge:

- Leskovec, J., & Mcauley, J. J. (2012). Learning to discover social circles in ego networks. In *Advances in neural information processing systems*.
- Zachary, W. W. (1977). An information flow model for conflict and fission in small groups. Journal of anthropological research, 33(4).

8
Social Networks and Going Viral

Network analysis is often used to understand the behavior of groups of people. Relationships within a group of people form a kind of network—a **social network**. Social networks are some of the longest-studied in network science, and provide some of the results most directly applicable to everyday life. This chapter will introduce you to the elementary results in social network analysis.

Topics in this chapter include the following:

- **Social networks**: The history of social networks in network science
- **Strong and weak ties**: How to interpret and quantify the intensity of relationships
- **The small world problem**: Understanding how very large networks can be spanned by relatively short paths
- **Contagion**: How information, diseases, and anything else spreads over networks

Social networks

The defining feature of social networks is that nodes represent people. The networks themselves can represent anything from small informal friend groups to entire societies.

Edges in a social network represent a type of relationship between people. Often, this relationship is friendship or communication. However, it can also be something as abstract as the similarity in their video streaming behavior. Just imagine; you might never have met someone, but you could be the only two people in the world who enjoy watching videos of sleeping hippos. That is certainly a kind of relationship!

Many of the tools of network science come from the study of social networks in sociology. The sociologists, Jacob L. Moreno and Helen Hall Jennings, developed the techniques of sociometry, a precursor to modern social network analysis and network science (Moreno And Jennings, 1934).

Social networks deserve special attention because common human behaviors result in characteristic types of network structure. Also, the structure of a social network has important implications for social processes, including the following:

- Finding job opportunities
- The spread of ideas
- The spread of disease
- Health behaviors

Strong and weak ties

In social networks, not all relationships are created equal. You might cosign a loan application for your sibling, but probably not for your cousin's babysitter's dentist's chimney sweep. In sociology, the strength of a relationship is captured by the concept of **tie strength**. In this context, a tie is some kind of an interpersonal relationship, and the strength is any measure of how intense or intimate that relationship is.

In 1973, the sociologist Mark Granovetter described the importance of weak ties in bridging different communities. If all ties within a community are strong, then any ties between communities must be weak. He described this phenomenon as the strength of weak ties. By bridging different communities, weak ties make it possible to find information from distant parts of a network. But how do we measure tie strength?

Tie strength

One approach to measuring tie strength was described in `Chapter 2`, *Working with Networks in NetworkX*. This section will build on that example using the Zachary karate club network (1977). The code to load the network is reproduced from `Chapter 2`, *Working with Networks in NetworkX*, as follows:

```
G = nx.karate_club_graph()
# Annotate with splinter club label
member_club = [
    0, 0, 0, 0, 0, 0, 0, 0, 1, 1,
    0, 0, 0, 0, 1, 1, 0, 0, 1, 0,
```

```
    1, 0, 1, 1, 1, 1, 1, 1, 1, 1,
    1, 1, 1, 1]
nx.set_node_attributes(G, dict(enumerate(member_club)), 'club')
# Find internal and external edges
internal = [
 (v, w) for v, w in G.edges
 if G.nodes[v]['club'] == G.nodes[w]['club']]
external = [
 (v, w) for v, w in G.edges
 if G.nodes[v]['club'] != G.nodes[w]['club']]
```

By the definition of community, individuals in the same community are more likely to have common friends than those in different communities. So, as in `Chapter 2`, *Working with Networks in NetworkX*, the number of common friends can be used to construct a measure of tie strength as follows:

```
def tie_strength(G, v, w):
    # Get neighbors of nodes v and w in G
    v_neighbors = set(G.neighbors(v))
    w_neighbors = set(G.neighbors(w))
    # Return size of the set intersection
    return 1 + len(v_neighbors & w_neighbors)
```

The following code calculates the tie strength of each edge and stores it in `strength`:

```
strength = dict(
    ((v,w), tie_strength(G, v, w))
    for v, w in G.edges())
```

Bridge span

Tie strength can also be quantified by considering the effect of removing an edge from the network. Nodes connected by an edge are always distance 1 apart (in an unweighted network). But if that edge is removed, its endpoints could be anywhere from distance 2 apart to entirely unconnected. This concept is captured by the **bridge span**, the network distance between an edge's endpoints if that edge is removed. Edges with large spans connect distant parts of a network, so they may be considered weak ties, despite playing an important role.

The following code calculates the span of each edge in the karate club network:

```
def bridge_span(G):
    # Get list of edges
    edges = G.edges()
    # Copy G
```

```
        G = nx.Graph(G)
        # Create result dict
        result = dict()
        for v, w in edges:
            # Temporarily remove edge
            G.remove_edge(v, w)
            # Find distance with edge removed
            try:
                d = nx.shortest_path_length(G, v, w)
                result[(v, w)] = d
            except nx.NetworkXNoPath:
                result[(v, w)] = float('inf')
            # Restore edge
            G.add_edge(v, w)
        return result

span = bridge_span(G)
```

Comparing strength and span

Let's look at the 10 strongest and 10 weakest edges in the karate club network. The following code prints these edges:

```
# Order edges by tie strength
ordered_edges = sorted(strength.items(), key=lambda x: x[1])
print('Edge\t Strength\tSpan\tInternal')
# Print 10 strongest
for e, edge_strength in ordered_edges[:10]:
    print('{:10}{}\t\t{}\t{}'.format(
        str(e), edge_strength, span[e], G.edges[e]['internal']))
print('...')
# Print 10 weakest
for e, edge_strength in ordered_edges[-10:]:
    print('{:10}{}\t\t{}\t{}'.format(
        str(e), edge_strength, span[e], G.edges[e]['internal']))
```

```
Edge Strength Span Internal
(0, 11) 1 inf internal
(0, 31) 1 3 external
(1, 30) 1 3 external
(2, 9) 1 3 external
(2, 27) 1 3 external
(2, 28) 1 3 external
(9, 33) 1 3 internal
(13, 33) 1 3 external
(19, 33) 1 3 external
```

```
(23, 25) 1 3 internal
...
(8, 32) 4 2 internal
(23, 33) 4 2 internal
(29, 33) 4 2 internal
(1, 2) 5 2 internal
(1, 3) 5 2 internal
(2, 3) 5 2 internal
(0, 2) 6 2 internal
(0, 3) 6 2 internal
(0, 1) 8 2 internal
(32, 33) 11 2 internal
```

The preceding output shows that the edges with low strength and high span are typically external, connecting club members who split into different splinter clubs. On the other hand, the high strength and low span edges are all internal, connecting club members who stayed together after the split.

The small world problem

In 1967, the social psychologists Jeffrey Travers and Stanley Milgram sent letters to groups of people in Wichita, Kansas, and Omaha, Nebraska. They also chose a single target individual in Massachusetts. Each letter recipient was instructed to forward their letter to an acquaintance who was most likely to know the target individual. Many of the letters reached the target, and the researchers were able to find out how many steps it took. The medium number of hops was six, hence, the common phrase **six degrees of separation**.

Ring networks

Typically, most of an individual's acquaintances are others who live in the same area. If every individual was only acquainted with others who lived near them, you would expect it to require many more than six hops to send a message from Kansas to Massachusetts, because each hop could only cross a short distance. Such a network can be modeled as a k-ring: nodes arranged around a circle, with each node connected to the nearest k/2 nodes on each side. The following example creates and visualizes a four-ring using the `watts_strogatz_graph()` function (which will be discussed later in the section).

```
G_small_ring = nx.watts_strogatz_graph(16, 4, 0)
pos = nx.circular_layout(G_small_ring)
nx.draw_networkx(G_small_ring, pos=pos, with_labels=False)
```

The preceding code uses `circular_layout()` (discussed in `Chapter 11`, *Visualization*) to visualize the network with the nodes around a circle:

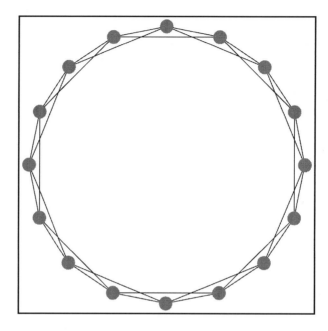

Four-ring network with 16 nodes

To connect two nodes in the preceding example requires passing around the edge of the circle, skipping at most every other node. Even in this very small network, the typical network distance is quite high compared to the six degrees that Travers and Milgram found.

The following code finds the mean shortest path and mean clustering in a more realistically sized 4000 node 10-ring:

```
G_ring = nx.watts_strogatz_graph(4000, 10, 0)
nx.average_shortest_path_length(G_ring)
200.45011252813202

nx.average_clustering(G_ring)
0.6666666666666546
```

This network has an average 200 degrees of separation, much bigger than six! It also has a fairly large mean clustering coefficient of 0.67, showing that a node's neighbors tend to be connected to each other.

A real social network

Let's see how the preceding results compare to a real social network (McAuley & Leskovec, 2012). The following code loads the network and calculates the mean shortest path and mean clustering:

```
# Load data file into network
from pathlib import Path
data_dir = Path('.') / 'data'
G_social =
nx.read_edgelist(
        data_dir / 'mcauley2012' /
     'facebook_combined.txt')

nx.average_shortest_path_length(G_social)
3.6925068496963913

nx.average_clustering(G_social)
0.6055467186200876
```

The clustering is very similar to the ring network model, but the mean shortest path is much smaller. There appears to be a paradox: we expect long path lengths in highly clustered networks, but highly clustered social networks seem to have very small path lengths.

Random networks

To investigate this mystery, let's consider a different kind of network. In this network, we start with a k-ring, but randomly rewire the endpoints of each edge. The result is a network with the same number of nodes and edges, but a random structure, demonstrated as follows:

```
G_small_random = nx.watts_strogatz_graph(16, 4, 1)
pos = nx.circular_layout(G_small_random)
nx.draw_networkx(G_small_random, pos=pos, with_labels=False)
```

Running the preceding code, we can see that randomization has added shortcut edges that cut across the ring:

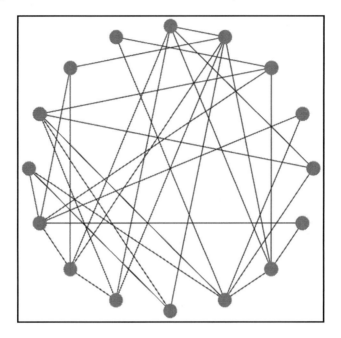

Rewired four-ring with 16 nodes

Now, let's examine the properties of a rewired 4000 node 10-ring:

```
G_random = nx.watts_strogatz_graph(4000, 10, 1)
nx.average_shortest_path_length(G_random)
3.867353963490873

nx.average_clustering(G_random)
0.0024101789958407643
```

The mean shortest path is very close to the real social network! ... but the mean clustering is now nearly 0. So far, the models we've seen achieve short paths or high clustering, but not both. How do real social networks do it?!

Watts-Strogatz networks

In 1998, Duncan Watts and Steven Strogatz found a way to model networks with both high clustering and short path lengths. It begins with a ring network, but only rewires some of the edges. In fact, this is exactly what the `watts_strogatz_graph()` function we've been using does, and the third parameter specifies the fraction of edges to rewire. The following code calculates the average shortest path and average clustering for a range of rewiring probabilities:

```
path = []
clustering = []
# Try a range of rewiring probabilities
p = [10**(x) for x in range(-6, 1)]
for p_i in p:
    path_i = []
    clustering_i =[]
    # Create 10 models for each probability
    for n in range(10):
        G = nx.watts_strogatz_graph(1000, 10, p_i)
        path_i.append(nx.average_shortest_path_length(G))
        clustering_i.append(nx.average_clustering(G))
    # Average the properties for each p_i
    path.append(sum(path_i) / len(path_i))
    clustering.append(sum(clustering_i) / len(clustering_i))
```

The results of the following code are stored in the `path` and `clustering` lists. Using the `semilogx()` function from `matplotlib.pyplot`, the following code visualizes how these values change as the rewiring probability ranges from 0 to 1:

```
# Plot the results
fig, ax = plt.subplots()
for spine in ax.spines.values():
    spine.set_visible(True)
plt.semilogx(p, [x / path[0] for x in path], label='Mean Path / Initial')
plt.semilogx(p, [x / clustering[0] for x in clustering], label='Clustering
/ Initial')
plt.tick_params(axis='both', which='major', labelsize=16)
plt.xlabel('Rewiring Probability p', fontsize=16)
plt.legend(fontsize=16)
```

The `semilogx()` function uses a logarithmic scale for the x-axis. Often in network science, values change so quickly that visualizing them on a linear scale results in an initial value that immediately drops to a final value. The `semilogx()` function can uncover behavior that might be lost using a linear axis. The `pyplot` package also offers the `semilogy()` and `loglog()` functions for using other logarithmic axes.

Running the preceding code gives us the following plot:

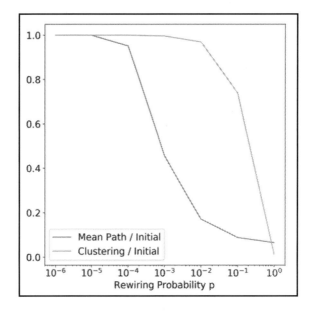

Change in network properties with rewiring probability

As the amount of rewiring increases, both the mean clustering and the mean shortest path drop, as we've already seen. However, the interesting thing happens at intermediate values. The path length becomes short at very low rewiring values, while the drop in clustering only happens at larger rewiring values. In other words, rewiring a very small fraction of edges creates bridges that connect remote parts of the network and drastically reduce the mean shortest path, without altering the clustering.

Contagion – how things spread

So far, it's been a lot of fun calculating numbers and arranging them into nifty little tables, but what's the point? It turns out that properties such as clustering and path length are incredibly important for social processes! In particular, they're important for contagion: the spread of ideas, disease, or anything else that moves from person to person. Understanding how network structure influences the spread of diseases and ideas makes it possible to

Simple contagion

A **simple contagion** is a social process in which each individual becomes infected after a single exposure. Simple contagions are good models for highly contagious diseases, or the spread of uncontroversial information.

The following code simulates a single step of a simple contagion. Infection status is stored in the infected node attribute. At each time step, the neighbors of all currently infected nodes are marked as infected:

```
def propagate_simple(G):
    to_infect = set([])
    # Find infected nodes
    for v in G.nodes():
        if G.nodes[v]['infected'] == False:
        # Mark all neighbors for infection
        for w in nx.neighbors(G, v):
            if G.nodes[w]['infected']:
                to_infect.add(v)
                break
    # Infect marked nodes
    for v in to_infect:
        G.nodes[v]['infected'] = True
```

Let's see how simple contagions spread through a ring network. We begin with two infected nodes:

```
nx.set_node_attributes(
    G_small_ring,
    dict((i, False) for i in range(16)),
    'infected')
for i in range(2):
    G_small_ring.nodes[i]['infected'] = True
    plt.figure(figsize=(7.5, 2.5))
```

The contagion is then allowed to spread from infected nodes to neighbors twice:

```
for i in range(3):
    plt.subplot(1, 3, i + 1)
    node_color = [
        '#bfbf7f' if G_small_ring.nodes[v]['infected'] else '#9f9fff'
        for v in G_small_ring.nodes]
    nx.draw_networkx(
    G_small_ring,
    pos=nx.circular_layout(G_small_ring),
    node_color=node_color)
    propagate_complex(G_small_ring)
```

```
        plt.title("Step {}".format(i))
    plt.tight_layout()
```

The preceding code visualizes the initial network and the network after each step:

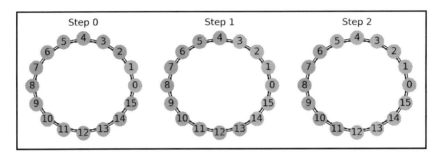

Simple contagion on a ring network

Now, let's compare the preceding to the spread of a simple contagion on a random network. Again, we begin by infecting two nodes.

```
nx.set_node_attributes(
    G_small_random,
    dict((i, False) for i in range(16)),
    'infected')
for i in range(2):
    G_small_random.nodes[i]['infected'] = True
```

The code to simulate the contagion is the same as the previous and is omitted. Simulating a simple contagion on a rewired ring gives the following:

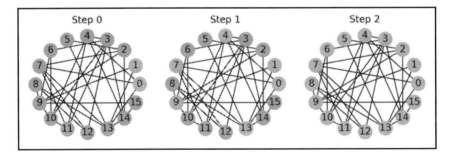

Simple contagion on a rewired ring network

After two time steps, the contagion has spread to the entire random network, while it has spread to less than half of the ring network. The spread of a simple contagion depends primarily on the path lengths present in the network, and the long path lengths of a ring network slow the spread.

Complex contagion

Not all contagions are spread after a single exposure. Less contagious diseases might need multiple exposures to infect an individual. Similarly, controversial ideas or behaviors, for example, joining a social movement or adopting a new technology, might require an individual to get recommendations from multiple friends multiple friends. Such contagions are called **complex contagions** (Centola & Macy, 2007). The following code simulates a complex contagion by only infecting a node if it has two or more infected neighbors:

```
def propagate_complex(G):
    to_infect = set([])
    # Find uninfected nodes
    for v in G.nodes():
        if G.nodes[v]['infected'] == False:
            infected_neighbors = 0
            # Count infected neighbors
            for w in nx.neighbors(G, v):
                if G.nodes[w]['infected']:
                    infected_neighbors += 1
            # Remember nodes with 2+ infected neighbors
            if infected_neighbors >= 2:
                to_infect.add(v)
    # Infect new nodes
    for v in to_infect:
        G.nodes[v]['infected'] = True
```

The following example simulates a complex contagion on a ring network. The following code initializes two nodes to the infected state:

```
nx.set_node_attributes(
    G_small_ring,
    dict((i, False) for i in range(16)),
    'infected')
for i in range(2):
    G_small_ring.nodes[i]['infected'] = True
```

The next step is to call `propagate_complex()` twice and visualize the output:

```
plt.figure(figsize=(7.5, 2.5))
for i in range(3):
    # Visualize
    plt.subplot(1, 3, i + 1)
    node_color = [
        '#bfbf7f' if G_small_ring.nodes[v]['infected'] else '#9f9fff'
        for v in G_small_ring.nodes]
    nx.draw_networkx(
        G_small_ring,
        pos=nx.circular_layout(G_small_ring),
        node_color=node_color)
    # Propagate the contagion
    propagate_complex(G_small_ring)
    plt.title("Step {}".format(i))
plt.tight_layout()
```

The preceding code shows the initial ring network, and the network after each step of complex contagion:

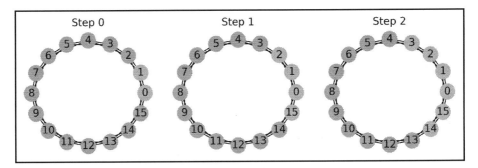

Complex contagion on a ring network

Compare this diagram to the following diagram, showing two steps of complex contagion on a rewired ring (the code is similar to the preceding code and is omitted):

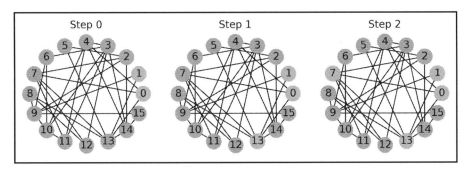

Complex contagion on a rewired ring network

The results for the complex contagion are strikingly different from those for the simple contagion. While the contagion still spreads slowly for the ring network, it doesn't spread at all on the random network! Complex contagions require high clustering to spread, which prevents their spread on random networks.

Summary

Social networks are one of the most compelling applications of network science. From the early days of sociometry to the more recent social network analysis, concepts from network science have helped uncover insights about groups of people and how they interact. Tie strength can be used to find weak ties that predict how communities might split and that enable information to spread across distant regions of a network. Small world networks resolve the paradox of small paths across networks of local connections. All of these structural properties have important implications for contagions: the spread of things such as ideas and diseases across groups of people. The concepts learned in this chapter are crucial for understanding how people behave and interact in groups. If you liked simulating contagions in this chapter, you'll love the next one! It's all about simulating network formation and behavior on networks.

References

The following is a list of resources that you can consider to get further knowledge:

- Granovetter, M. S. (1977). The strength of weak ties. In Social networks. Academic Press.
- Moreno, J. L., & Jennings, H. H. (1934). Who Shall Survive? Nervous and Mental Disease.
- Travers, J., & Milgram, S. (1967). The small world problem. *Psychology Today*, 1(1).
- Watts, D. J., & Strogatz, S. H. (1998). Collective dynamics of 'small-world' networks. Nature, 393(6684).
- Zachary, W. W. (1977). An information flow model for conflict and fission in small groups. Journal of anthropological research, 33(4).

Simulation and Analysis

9

Network structure is intimately related to the processes that occur in networked systems. Different processes create different structures, and different structures influence networked processes. Simulations can be used to generate synthetic networks. These networks can be used to study how structure forms in real systems. Real or synthetic networks can also be used to simulate processes that occur on those networks, to understand the influence of structure on those processes. This chapter introduces several common synthetic network models, as well as an example of simulating networked processes using agent-based modeling.

In this chapter, we will cover the following topics:

- **Watts-Strogatz networks**: Simulating small worlds by adding random shortcuts to locally-clustered networks
- **Preferential attachment**: How the rich getting richer creates scale-free heavy-tailed networks
- **Configuration models**: How to create synthetic networks that mimic the properties of real data
- **Agent-based models**: How to simulate behaviors and processes occurring within networks

Watts-Strogatz and small worlds

The small-world problem (discussed in Chapter 8, *Social Networks and Going Viral*) asks how it is possible for distant people to be connected by short paths, even when everyone's connections are local (Travers & Milgram, 1967). Duncan Watts and Steven Strogatz (1998) developed a class of networks to explain this behavior. The networks begin as k-rings: nodes placed around a circle, with each node connected to its nearest k neighbors. Then, with probability p, each node's edges are moved to a randomly selected other node. These **rewirings** create **shortcuts** across the network. Even a small number of shortcuts greatly reduces the distances between nodes in the network, resolving the small-world problem.

The following code uses the `NetworkX` function `watts_strogatz_graph()` to generate Watts-Strogatz small-world networks with p=0, p=0.1, and p=1:

```
plt.figure(figsize=(7.5, 2.25))
for i, p in enumerate([0.0, 0.1, 1.0]):
    # Generate the graph
    G = nx.watts_strogatz_graph(12, 6, p)
    # Create layout and draw
    plt.subplot(1, 3, i + 1)
    pos = nx.circular_layout(G)
    nx.draw_networkx(G, pos=pos)
    plt.title("p = {:0.1f}".format(p))
```

This code loops over three rewiring probabilities and visualizes the resulting Watts-Strogatz networks:

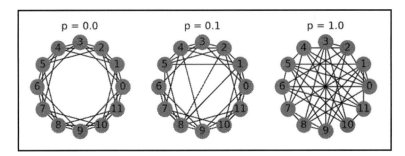

Watts-Strogatz small-world networks

In some cases, rewiring can result in two components in a Watts-Strogatz network becoming disconnected. A disconnected network can be an unnecessary complication. The Newman-Watts-Strogatz network is a variation that guarantees that the resulting network will be connected. It is similar to the original version, but leaves a copy of the original edge in place for each edge that is rewired. These networks can be created using the `newman_watts_strogatz_graph()` function, shown as follows:

```
plt.figure(figsize=(7.5, 2.25))
for i, p in enumerate([0.0, 0.1, 1.0]):
    # Generate the graph
    G = nx.newman_watts_strogatz_graph(12, 6, p)
    # Create layout and draw
    plt.subplot(1, 3, i + 1)
    pos = nx.circular_layout(G)
    nx.draw_networkx(G, pos=pos)
    plt.title("p = {:0.1f}".format(p))
```

The preceding code visualizes the three resulting networks, producing the following:

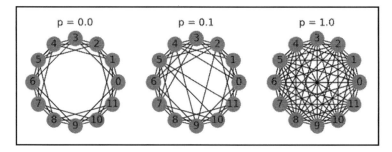

Newman-Watts-Strogatz small-world networks

Preferential attachment and heavy-tailed networks

From the internet to airport trips, many networks are characterized by a few nodes with many connections, and many nodes with very few connections. These networks are called **heavy-tailed** because, when a histogram of the node degrees is drawn, the high-connectivity nodes form a tail.

There are many ways to generate heavy-tailed networks, but one of the most widely-used is the Barabási-Albert **preferential attachment** model (Albert & Barabási, 1999). The preferential attachment model mimics processes where the rich get richer. Every time a node is added, it is randomly connected to existing nodes, with high-degree nodes being more likely.

In NetworkX, the barabasi_albert_graph() function generates preferential attachment networks. The following code shows an example of such a network with 35 nodes:

```
G_preferential_35 = nx.barabasi_albert_graph(35, 1)
pos = nx.spring_layout(G_preferential_35, k=0.1)
nx.draw_networkx(G_preferential_35, pos)
```

This code creates the network and then visualizes it using a force-directed layout, producing the following:

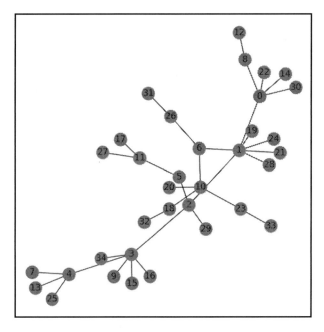

35-Node Barabási-Albert preferential attachment network

The structure of a preferential attachment network is even more apparent with a larger number of nodes. The following example uses 500 nodes:

```
G_preferential_500 = nx.barabasi_albert_graph(500, 1)
pos = nx.spring_layout(G_preferential_500)
nx.draw_networkx(G_preferential_500, pos, node_size=0, with_labels=False)
```

Running this code visualizes the larger network:

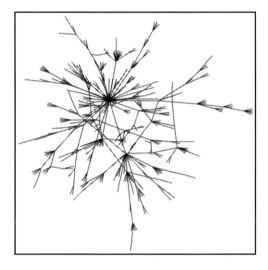

500-Node Barabási-Albert preferential attachment network

The heavy tails of these networks can be seen by plotting their degree distributions. The following function plots the degree distribution of a network:

```
def plot_degree_hist(G, title):
    """Plot histogram of node degrees."""
    plt.hist(dict(nx.degree(G)).values(), bins=range(1, 11))
    # Label axes
    plt.xlabel('Degree')
    plt.ylabel('Count')
    plt.title(title)
```

Using this function, the following code visualizes the degree distributions for the 35-node and 500-node preferential attachment networks:

```
plt.figure(figsize=(7.5, 3.75))
ax = plt.subplot(1,2,1)
plot_degree_hist(G_preferential_35, '35 Nodes')
for spine in ax.spines.values():
    spine.set_visible(True)
ax = plt.subplot(1,2,2)
for spine in ax.spines.values():
    spine.set_visible(True)
plot_degree_hist(G_preferential_500, '500 Nodes')
plt.tight_layout()
```

This code produces the following visualization:

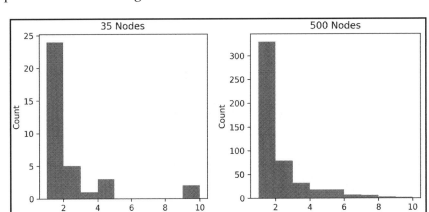

Degree distributions for 35-node and 500-node Barabási-Albert networks

Preferential attachment networks exhibit an additional property: they are **scale-free**. Degree distributions in scale-free networks follow a power law, which results in a similar structure at different scales. One way to see this is by comparing the preceding histograms. Despite very different scales, they have similar shapes.

Configuration models

When you need a synthetic network to resemble an existing network, **configuration models** might be the way to go. Given an input network, they produce a new network with the same number of nodes, each with the same degree. The edges of the new network are created randomly, in a way that preserves node degree.

 Configuration models and other methods for constructing synthetic networks based on real data can be used to protect privacy. For example, online social networks can release configuration models based on their true member network to allow researchers to study the properties of those networks without having access to members' private data.

As an example, we can use a configuration model to create a synthetic network based on the karate club network. The following code shows exactly how to do this, using the configuration_model() function in the degree_seq package:

```
# Find degrees of karate club nodes
G_karate = nx.karate_club_graph()
```

```
degree_sequence = dict(nx.degree(G_karate)).values()
# Generate a random network with the same node degrees
G_configuration = nx.degree_seq.configuration_model(degree_sequence)
nx.draw_networkx(G_configuration)
```

The preceding code uses degree() to get the degrees of nodes in the karate club network, and configuration_model() to produce a random network with the same node degrees, resulting in the following:

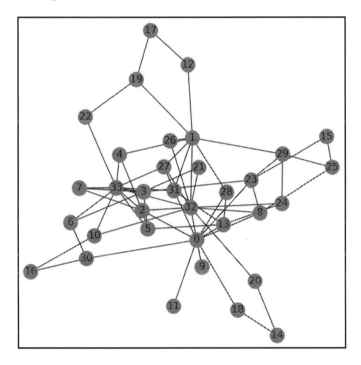

Configuration model network based on the Zachary karate club

Agent-based models

Beyond just looking at how network structure is created, simulations can be used to explore the processes that take place on top of an existing network. Such simulations can be used to anticipate the effects of changing network structure on a complex system, or to predict problems, such as traffic jams and power outages.

This section introduces one type of simulation: **agent-based modeling**. Agent-based modeling is a common technique in complex systems that simulates multiple objects called agents. Each agent is described by its state. Depending on the application, a state might be a single number, or a complex data structure. As the simulation proceeds, each agent interacts with other agents, and their states are updated based on those interactions. Sometimes, all agents are allowed to interact with all other agents. But this is a book about networks, and in a network setting, agents are nodes in a network and are only allowed to interact with their neighbors.

As a concrete example, agent-based modeling can be used to simulate a group of people who have made noisy observations of some quantity, such as the temperature, and wish to estimate the true value of that quantity. When the individuals can improve their estimates by communicating with each other, this process is known as **social learning**. One of the simplest methods is for each agent to average its neighbors estimates and use that average as its new estimate (DeGroot, 1974; Golub & Jackson, 2010). The following function generates an initial set of agent beliefs by adding normally distributed noise to a true value:

```
def initial_beliefs(G, true_value=0, std=15):
    """Generate estimates of a true value with normally-distributed
errors."""
    beliefs = dict(
        (v, random.gauss(true_value, std))
        for v in G.nodes())
    return beliefs
```

We use the preceding function by passing it a `Graph` with nodes corresponding to agents, and the true value used to generate observations for the agents:

```
beliefs = initial_beliefs(G_karate, true_value=42)
```

In their quest to uncover the answer to life, the universe, and everything, our agents now have a range of values, more or less centered around 42.

The simulation process can be implemented by defining a function that takes current beliefs as input and returns an updated set of beliefs. The following code simulates one round of social learning:

```
def learning_step(G, beliefs):
    """Update each node's beliefs based on its neighbors' beliefs."""
    new_beliefs = dict()
    for v in G.nodes():
        # Include old belief in average
        total = beliefs[v]
        count = 1
        # Update average based on each neighbor
```

```
        for w in G.neighbors(v):
            total += beliefs[w]
            count += 1
        # Calculate average for node w
        new_beliefs[v] = total / count
    return new_beliefs
```

Running `learning_step()` multiple times simulates the convergence of beliefs over several rounds of social learning. Plotting the value of each agent's state over time visualizes the convergence of beliefs as the agents interact with each other. The following function simulates several rounds of social learning on a given network, and plots the evolution of agent states:

```
def plot_beliefs(G, initial_beliefs, true_value=0, steps=10):
    """Plot change in beliefs over time."""
    current_beliefs = dict(initial_beliefs)
    beliefs = [current_beliefs]
    # Create dicts of x and y values for each node
    x = dict((v, list()) for v in G.nodes())
    y = dict((v, list()) for v in G.nodes())
    # Repeatedly update beliefs
    for i in range(steps + 1):
        for v in G.nodes():
            x[v].append(i)
            y[v].append(current_beliefs[v])
        if i < steps:
            current_beliefs = learning_step(G, current_beliefs)
            beliefs.append(current_beliefs)
    # Plot evolution of each node's beliefs
    for v in G.nodes():
        plt.plot(x[v], y[v], 'b-', alpha=0.3, linewidth=2)
    # Plot mean value
    mean_value = sum(initial_beliefs.values()) / len(initial_beliefs)
    plt.plot([0, steps], [mean_value, mean_value], 'k:')
    # Add spines to plot
    ax = plt.gca()
    for spine in ax.spines.values():
        spine.set_visible(True)
    plt.xlim([0, steps])
    plt.ylim([22, 62])
```

In putting all of the preceding code together, the following code performs an agent-based simulation of social learning on several different networks, all starting from the same initial beliefs:

```
# dict of networks
networks = {
```

```
        'Karate Club': G_karate,
        'Configuration Model': G_configuration,
        'Preferential Attachment': nx.barabasi_albert_graph(34, 1),
        'Ring': nx.watts_strogatz_graph(34, 6, 0),
        'Watts-Strogatz (p=0.3)': nx.watts_strogatz_graph(34, 6, 0.1),
        'Watts-Strogatz (p=1)': nx.watts_strogatz_graph(34, 6, 1)}

# Simulate and plot results for each network
for i, (title, G) in enumerate(networks.items()):
    plt.subplot(3, 2, i + 1)
    plt.title(title)
    plot_beliefs(G, beliefs, 42)
plt.tight_layout()
```

The preceding code creates six plots, one for each network, shown as follows. In each plot, there is one line per agent, showing the evolution of their beliefs over time:

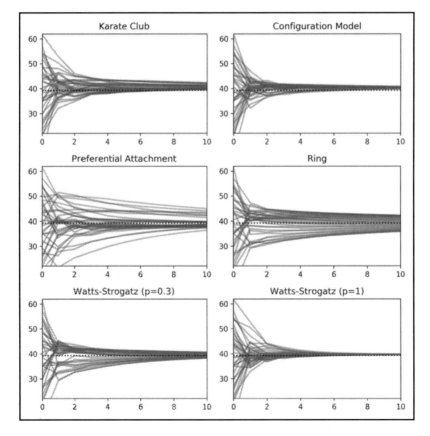

Social learning on different network topologies

All of the preceding examples converge toward the general vicinity of the true value (42), but the details of how they converge vary drastically between different network structures. The karate club network and the configuration model based on it look similar, but they are not exactly the same. Note that they both converge to a value slightly off from the mean, due to some nodes having higher influence.

The preferential attachment network converges very slowly, and allows incorrect beliefs to persist if they are held by highly-central agents.

The ring network converges slowly, but uniformly, and to approximately the correct value. The totally random Watts-Strogatz network (p=1) also converges to an approximately correct value, but more quickly. The p=0.2 Watts-Strogatz network falls somewhere between them.

In this simple social learning setting, the correctness of the result turns out to depend only on the degree distribution (Golub & Jackson, 2010). If all nodes have the same degree, the network will always converge to the true average of the initial values. The speed of convergence, on the other hand, depends on the structure of the network, in particular, a property called eigenvalue gap, which is beyond the scope of this book, but can easily be found using linear algebra.

Summary

This chapter has shown us how simulations can be used to better understand both the processes that create network structure and the processes that are influenced by network structure. The Watts-Strogatz model creates small-world networks by adding random shortcuts to a highly-clustered ring network. Preferential attachment creates heavy-tailed, scale-free networks, where a few nodes have most of the connections. Configuration models are used to construct synthetic networks with properties similar to real networks. Finally, this chapter showed how agent-based modeling can be used to simulate a social learning process occurring on an existing network structure. In the next chapter, you'll learn about working with data that represents objects in space or time.

References

The following is a list of resources that you can consider to get further knowledge:

- Barabási, A. L., & Albert, R. (1999). Emergence of scaling in random networks. Science, 286(5439).
- DeGroot, M. H. (1974). Reaching a consensus. *Journal of the American Statistical Association*, 69(345).
- Golub, B., & Jackson, M. O. (2010). Naive learning in social networks and the wisdom of crowds. *American Economic Journal: Microeconomics*, 2(1).
- Travers, J., & Milgram, S. (1967). The small world problem. *Psychology Today*, 1(1).
- Watts, D. J., & Strogatz, S. H. (1998). Collective dynamics of 'small-world' networks. Nature, 393(6684).

Networks in Space and Time 10

Throughout this book so far, nodes have existed outside of any particular time or space. In visualizations, nodes have been placed on a two-dimensional space (pages), but only because it would be difficult to tell them apart if they were all on top of each other. In some cases, nodes truly are associated with a particular spatial location or a particular time. In these cases, additional techniques can be helpful for visualizing and analyzing networks. This chapter describes some of the special techniques needed for networks in space and time and applies them to real-world examples, including airports and links on Wikipedia.

Topics in this chapter include the following:

- **Locations and events**: Explaining how networks can be used to represent data with temporal and spatial properties
- **Networks in space**: Visualizing and analyzing relationships between locations
- **Networks in time**: Visualizing and analyzing how relationships change over time

Locations and events

Networks can represent just about any kind of relationship, and that includes relationships between times or between places. In both cases, network properties become influenced by the real-world constraints of time and place. Similarly, visualizations of these networks can use the space of a screen or page to convey useful information about spatial and temporal relationships.

Networks in space

Nodes are associated with specific geographic locations in many important networks, for example the following:

- Electrical grids
- Road networks
- Airports linked by direct flights
- Telecommunication lines

The edges in these networks are physical objects and have physical properties that can influence the behavior of the system represented by the network. One weight measure isn't always enough. For example, when an edge represents a fiber optic telecommunications cable, it is important to consider both the physical length of the cable and the bandwidth (capacity) of the cable. The former influences how long signals take to travel along the cable, while the latter influences how much data it can handle (and both of these influences cost!). Not to mention that a telecommunication cable is only useful if it connects two physical locations with people who want to talk to each other!

Gravity models

Length in spatial networks is often associated with cost, whether that's the monetary cost of laying a cable, or the time spent on a long flight. As a result, these networks tend to be built out of many short edges, and fewer long edges. Similarly, some types of networks exhibit edge weights that decrease with the length of the edge. For example, the number of passengers traveling directly between two airports generally decreases with distance. So, if an edge is high-weight, it could be just because it's short, or it could be because something more interesting is going on. A technique called a **gravity model** can be used to correct for length when comparing two-edge weights.

Gravity models assume that, on average, the strength of an interaction between two points will be inversely proportional to the distance between them squared. They're called gravity models because, in physics, the gravitational attraction between two bodies follows a similar law (at least until you get to grad school). The strength of an interaction is also assumed to increase proportionally to some mass-like property of each of the nodes, such as the total traffic through an airport. The following section demonstrates how to apply a simple gravity model to airport traffic.

Working with spatial data

This section will give examples of working with spatial data in NetworkX. In particular, the examples analyze direct flights in the continental US in 2018. In this network, nodes represent airports and edges represent passenger flow between those airports. This is a spatial network because the airports correspond to geographic locations and the distance spanned by each edge is relevant when analyzing the network. The following code loads the network row by row:

```
# Load data file into network
from pathlib import Path
data_dir = Path('.') / 'data'
G_air = nx.Graph()
with open(data_dir / 'BTS2018' / 'carrier.csv') as f:
    # Skip header
    next(f)
    # Loop through data rows
    for row in f:
        count, v, w, year, month = row.strip().split(',')
        count = int(count)
        if count == 0 or v == w:
            continue
        try:
            G_air.edges[v, w]['count'] += count
        except KeyError:
            G_air.add_edge(v, w, count=count)
```

The preceding code loads the airport traffic data, but not the geographic locations of the airports. We can use the airport code to match each airport to a latitude and longitude in the Global Airport Database (Partow, 2019). First, the latitude and longitude is loaded into a dictionary:

```
airport_lat_long = {}
with open(data_dir / 'partow' / 'GlobalAirportDatabase.txt') as f:
    for row in f:
        columns = row.strip().split(':')
        code = columns[1]
        lat = float(columns[14])
        long = float(columns[15])
        airport_lat_long[code] = (lat, long)
```

Next, each node is looked up in this dictionary, discarding nodes outside the continental US:

```
for v in list(G_air.nodes()):
    try:
        lat, long = airport_lat_long[v]
```

```
        if long == 0 or long < -128.6 or lat == 0 or lat < 23.5:
            G_air.remove_node(v)
            continue
        G_air.nodes[v]['lat'] = lat
        G_air.nodes[v]['long'] = long
    except KeyError:
        G_air.remove_node(v)
```

We also discard any disconnected airports by finding the largest connected component:

```
G_air = nx.subgraph(G_air, max(nx.connected_components(G_air), key=len))
```

Let's visualize the network using `draw_networkx()` as usual:

```
nx.draw_networkx(
    G_air, node_size=0, with_labels=False, edge_color='#666666', alpha=0.1)
```

This code hides nodes and labels, leaving only edges in order to reduce clutter. Unfortunately, running it still yields a meaningless hairball:

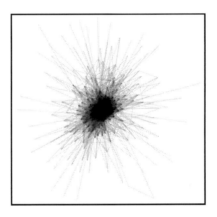

US air traffic network: force-directed layout

But there's still hope for our visualization! To start, the geographic location can be used to create a layout for the network visualization. Rather than using a built-in NetworkX layout function, this code creates the position dictionary `pos` manually:

```
import math
pos = dict()
for v in G_air.nodes:
    long = G_air.nodes[v]['long']
    lat = G_air.nodes[v]['lat']
    pos[v] = ((long + 90) * math.cos(2 * math.pi * lat / 360), lat)
```

The elements of `pos` correspond to x and y coordinates on the screen. On the other hand, latitude and longitude correspond to coordinates on a sphere. So, it is necessary to put in a little extra work to create a projection from latitude and longitude into x-y coordinates (if only the world was flat!).

> In the previous example, we simply scale the longitude according to the latitude, but there are better projections. The Python `cartopy` package provides a variety of projections and integrates well with `matplotlib`.

Now that the position of each node has been stored in `pos`, it can be passed to `draw_network_nodes()` and `draw_network_edges()` for visualization:

```
fig = plt.figure(figsize=(15,15))
ax = plt.subplot(1, 1, 1)
max_weight = max([G_air.edges[e]['count'] for e in G_air.edges])
nx.draw_networkx_nodes(G_air, pos=pos, node_color='#7f7fff', node_size=20)
for e in G_air.edges:
    alpha = G_air.edges[e]['count'] / max_weight
    nx.draw_networkx_edges(
        G_air, pos=pos, edgelist=[e], edge_color='#7f7fff', alpha=alpha,
arrows=False)
ax.set_aspect(1)
```

The preceding code draws each edge individually, which is necessary in order to draw them with different alpha parameters. The alpha is used to visualize how many passengers travel on direct flights between two airports. Doing so produces the following visualization:

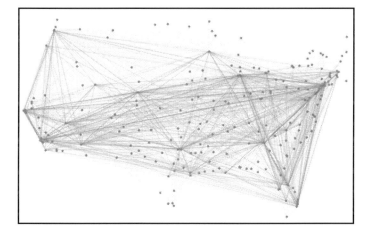

US air traffic network: geospatial layout

This visualization is much more informative than the earlier hairball. But, the analysis so far does not address an important question: if there is a high-weight edge between two airports, is it because those airports are conveniently close, or because there is some special relationship between those regions? The gravity model approach described earlier in this chapter can be used to adjust for distance.

Gravity model for air travel

Gravity models assume that, on average, the weight of an edge decreases with distance, so it is necessary to find the distance spanned by each edge. The following function finds an approximate distance using the **Haversine formula**, which assumes that the Earth is perfectly spherical:

```
def haversine(q, p):
    """Calculate the distance between two (lat, long) points."""
    R_km = 6371
    theta1 = q[1] * math.pi / 180
    phi1 = q[0] * math.pi / 180
    theta2 = p[1] * math.pi / 180
    phi2 = p[0] * math.pi / 180
    dphi = phi2 - phi1
    dtheta = theta2 - theta1
    a = (math.sin(dphi/2) * math.sin(dphi/2)
        + (math.cos(phi1) * math.cos(phi2)
            * math.sin(dtheta/2) * math.sin(dtheta/2)))
    c = 2 * math.atan2(math.sqrt(a), math.sqrt(1-a))
    d = R_km * c
    return d
```

There are several Python packages that implement the Haversine formula and more accurate geographic distance measures. These packages include `haversine` and `geopy`. The preceding function is included here for completeness.

Next, each edge is given a `distance` property to keep track of how far apart the endpoints are:

```
for v, w in G_air.edges:
    p_v = (G_air.nodes[v]['lat'], G_air.nodes[v]['long'])
    p_w = (G_air.nodes[w]['lat'], G_air.nodes[w]['long'])
    G_air.edges[v, w]['distance'] = haversine(p_v, p_w)
```

With the distances calculated, we now need the mass of each node. For this example, the total traffic through an airport will work, but depending on the application, other values could be used, such as population (or average squirrel size). The number of passengers traveling through an airport is just the weighted degree, and can be calculated as follows:

```
degree = G_air.degree(weight='count')
nx.set_node_attributes(G_air, dict(degree), 'degree')
```

We'll assume that the traffic across an edge is proportional to the product of the endpoints' masses divided by the square of the distance, but that leaves room for a constant multiplier. This multiplier can be calculated from the data. Usually, a linear regression model would be used to find the multiplier, but that is beyond the scope of this book, so we'll take a simpler approach. The following code considers each edge, and calculates which constant would be necessary in order to produce the observed edge weight:

```
g_list = []
for v, w in G_air.edges():
    if v >=w:
        continue
    try:
        count = G_air.edges[v, w]['count']
    except KeyError:
        g_list.append(0)
        continue
    distance = G_air.edges[v, w]['distance']
    v_degree = G_air.nodes[v]['degree']
    w_degree = G_air.nodes[w]['degree']
    g_list.append(count * distance**2 / v_degree / w_degree)
```

The preceding code stores the value calculated for each edge in `g_list`. Next, the values are combined into a single constant multiplier using the geometric mean:

```
g = 10**(sum([math.log10(g) for g in g_list]) / len(g_list))
```

The **geometric mean** is sometimes a better choice than the usual arithmetic mean when working with heavy-tailed data. The geometric mean is defined as the Nth root of the product of N values, but is equivalent to the preceding logarithmic formula.

The `g` multiplier can now be used to predict how much traffic should cross each edge based solely on the traffic through the endpoints and their distance from each other. The difference between the expected traffic and the actual traffic is called the **residual**. A positive residual indicates that an edge has more traffic than would be expected for its distance.

The following code calculates the residuals and adds them to each edge as a property:

```
for v, w in G_air.edges:
    if v == w:
        continue
    count = G_air.edges[v, w]['count']
    # Calculate expected weight
    expected = (
        g * G_air.nodes[v]['degree']
        * G_air.nodes[w]['degree']
        / G_air.edges[v, w]['distance']**2)
    G_air.edges[v, w]['expected'] = expected
    # Calculate residual
    G_air.edges[v, w]['residual'] = count - expected
    G_air.edges[v, w]['log_residual'] = math.log10(count) -
math.log10(expected)
```

Residual network

Using the residuals, it is possible to produce a **residual network**, consisting only of the edges that exceed their expected traffic. This network represents, in some ways, the most important airport connections. The residual network can be found by storing the edges in a list and using the edge_subgraph() method of the Graph class:

```
residual_edges = [e for e in G_air.edges if G_air.edges[e]['log_residual']
> 0]
G_residual = G_air.edge_subgraph(residual_edges)
# Keep the largest connected component
G_residual = nx.subgraph(G_residual,
max(nx.connected_components(G_residual), key=len))
```

The residual network is visualized just as before:

```
fig = plt.figure(figsize=(15,15))
ax = plt.subplot(1, 1, 1)
max_weight = max([G_residual.edges[e]['log_residual'] for e in
G_residual.edges])
nx.draw_networkx_nodes(G_residual, pos=pos, node_color='#7f7fff',
node_size=20)
for e in G_residual.edges:
    alpha = G_residual.edges[e]['log_residual'] / max_weight
    nx.draw_networkx_edges(
        G_residual, pos=pos, edgelist=[e], edge_color='#7f7fff',
alpha=alpha, arrows=False)
ax.set_aspect(1)
```

The resulting visualization is much sparser than the previous geographic visualization, and is definitely better than the hairball we started with:

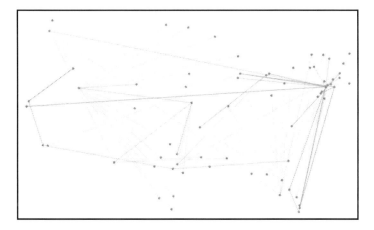

US air traffic: residual network

The preceding visualization makes it easy to identify important nodes and connections, many of which center around New York City, San Francisco, and Los Angeles, all important centers of commerce in the United States, as well as resort towns such as Wendover, Utah.

Network properties

The residual network calculated in the previous section can also be analyzed using the network measures discussed in Chapter 5, *The Small Scale – Nodes and Centrality*. The following code compares the average clustering of the original air transport network to that of the residual network:

```
nx.average_clustering(G_air)
0.6577002515250526

nx.average_clustering(G_residual)
0.03604529774872912
```

The original network has a very high clustering coefficient, typical of geographic infrastructural networks. On the other hand, the residual network, which has been adjusted to compensate for the effects of distance, exhibits a small clustering coefficient.

Networks in time

As we march forward toward the inevitable heat death of the universe, all things change, including networks. Networks that change in time are called **dynamic networks**. Network science is often concerned with how the structure of networks influences underlying systems. But, the reverse can be true as well: the processes that take place in a system can influence its network structure.

One approach to understanding how networks change over time is to look at snapshots. A **snapshot** is a network containing only the nodes and edges that were present at a specific point in time (like taking a picture). By taking snapshots at different times, network properties can be calculated at each point to understand how the network has evolved. One way to represent dynamic networks is to include all nodes and edges, but annotate them with the times them were present in the network. Snapshots can then be calculated by taking subsets of nodes and edges that match a particular point in time.

Layered networks

When interested in flows through a network over time, multiple snapshots of a network can be connected to each other. Each node then becomes multiple nodes – one for each snapshot. The copies of a particular node are then connected to each other by directed edges pointing from an earlier snapshot to a later snapshot. These edges represent flow over time. Such networks are an example of a **layered network**: each node and edge exists within a particular layer (in this case, the snapshot). Using a layered network makes it possible to identify flows between nodes when a path exists over time, but not within any single snapshot.

Working with time data

This section will demonstrate working with temporal data in NetworkX using links in the Dutch Wikipedia as an example. As articles are added and edited, new links appear and disappear, changing the network and its properties as time progresses.

The data (Ligtenberg & Pei, 2017) can be loaded from an edge list formatted file:

```
G_wiki = nx.read_edgelist(
    data_dir / 'ligtenberg2017' / 'wikilinks.csv',
    data=[('begin', int), ('end', int)],
    create_using=nx.MultiGraph)
len(G_wiki)
43509
```

The data parameter of `read_edgelist()` is used to read the beginning and ending time for each edge. `MultiGraph` is used because this particular data set allows edges to appear multiple times with different attributes. Times are stored as integers, which makes comparing times convenient. These integers, called **Unix timestamps**, represent seconds since the **epoch**, January 1, 1970 (coincidentally, the same as the number of seconds since someone first said "Back in the '60s..."). The full network contains over 43,509 nodes, which is a bit too many for us to work with here. Luckily, most of them are added over the course of time, so we can focus on the first few weeks of the data, when the network is still small.

The following function creates a snapshot of the network at a particular time, specified by the `date` parameter:

```python
import datetime
import time

def get_snapshot(G, date):
    """Convert date to integer timestamp."""
    dt = datetime.datetime.strptime(date, '%Y-%m-%d')
    timestamp = time.mktime(dt.timetuple())

    # Find edges that existed during timestamp
    snapshot_edges = []
    for e in G.edges:
        if G.edges[e]['begin'] <= timestamp and G_wiki.edges[e]['end'] >=
timestamp:
            snapshot_edges.append(e)

    # Create network from edges
    return nx.Graph(G.edge_subgraph(snapshot_edges))
```

The preceding code converts dates from a string to a Unix timestamp, and then creates a list of all edges that existed at the given time. Next, the `edge_subgraph()` method is used to create a new `Graph` containing only those edges. Using the function previously defined, it's now possible to visualize the network at different times over the course of six months using the following code:

```python
# Specify the dates to visualize
dates = [
    '2001-10-01',
    '2001-10-08',
    '2001-10-15',
    '2001-10-22',
    '2001-10-29',
    '2001-11-06',
]
```

```
# Create a figure
plt.figure(figsize=(10, 15))
# Visualize the network for each date
pos = None
for i, date in enumerate(reversed(dates)):
    # Get a snapshot of the network
    G = get_snapshot(G_wiki, date)
    # Create a subplot
    plt.subplot(3, 2, 6 - i)
    plt.title(date)
    # Calculate the layout
    pos = nx.spring_layout(G, pos=pos, k=0.09)
    # Visualize
    nx.draw_networkx(
        G, pos=pos, alpha=0.5, edge_color='#333333', node_size=0,
with_labels=False)
```

Running the preceding code produces the following visualization:

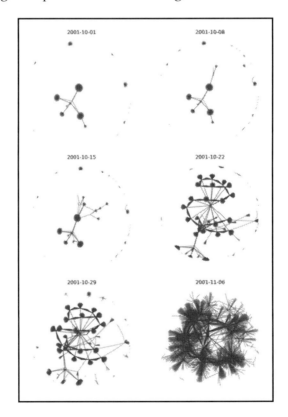

Links between Dutch Wikipedia articles

In the preceding visualization, only edges are drawn in order to reduce clutter. Regions of highly interconnected nodes appear as clumps of edges. Isolated groups of nodes appear around the edge of each visualization. Visualizing multiple snapshots of the network makes it possible to identify how the network structure evolves over time.

The evolution of network properties

Network snapshots can also be used to analyze the evolution of network properties over time. The following code creates snapshots of the Dutch Wikipedia at one-month intervals over the course of two years and calculates the average clustering of the network at each time:

```
year = 2001
month = 10
clustering = []
for i in range(24):
    date = '{}-{}-01'.format(year, month)
    G = get_snapshot(G_wiki, date)
    clustering.append(nx.average_clustering(G))
    # Update month and year
    month += 1
    if month > 12:
        month -= 12
        year += 1
```

The results of the preceding code can be plotted using the following code:

```
# Create figure
plt.figure(figsize=(7.5, 4))
ax = plt.subplot(1, 1, 1)
for spine in ax.spines.values():
    spine.set_visible(True)
# Plot clustering over time
plt.plot(clustering)
# Add labels and ticks
plt.ylabel('Average Clustering')
plt.xticks(
    [0, 6, 12, 18, 24],
    ['10/2001', '4/2002', '10/2002', '4/2003', '10/2003'])
plt.tight_layout()
```

The preceding code produces the following output:

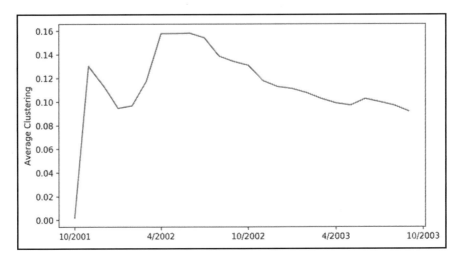

Evolution of clustering in Dutch Wikipedia links

From this visualization, it is easy to see that the clustering fluctuates between 0.1 and 0.16 for the first eight months, and then slowly decreases. In the context of Wikipedia, adding new articles decreases clustering, while adding links to existing articles increases clustering. These two effects competed as a large number of articles and links were added over the first few months. As the existing articles reached a stable state, with few new links, the steady addition of new articles caused the number of disconnected triads to grow faster than the number of connected triangles, resulting in a slow decline in clustering.

Summary

This chapter has shown how networks that exist in time or space can be represented, analyzed, and visualized in NetworkX. Such networks have additional constraints imposed by the physical realities of time and space. Spatial networks can be visualized using the actual locations of nodes. Gravity models can be used to compensate for different lengths when comparing edge properties. Networks that change over time can be analyzed by creating snapshots, and can possibly link those snapshots into a layered network. This chapter gave examples of working with temporal and spatial networks using US air traffic data and historical data on Dutch Wikipedia articles. The next chapter will cover some advanced visualization techniques in NetworkX.

References

The following is a list of resources that you can consider to get further knowledge:

- Ligtenberg, W., & Pei, Y. (2017). Introduction to a temporal graph benchmark. arXiv preprint arXiv:1703.02852.
- Partow, A. (2019). The Global Airport Database (Retrieved 14 April, 2019 from www.partow.net/miscellaneous/airportdatabase/index.html).

11
Visualization

Network visualizations are some of the most powerful tools for communicating information about relationships and connections. The vast amount of information in many networks can make it tricky to create clear visualizations, sometimes resulting in confusing **hairballs**. NetworkX is capable of producing many types of visualizations, going well beyond those seen in this book so far. This chapter covers some more advanced visualization techniques, including additional layouts and methods for focusing on the most important parts of a network.

The topics in this chapter include the following:

- **Beyond the hairball**: Understanding what makes a good visualization, the challenges of visualizing networks, and general approaches for addressing those challenges
- **Circular layout**: A simple method for visualizing smaller networks
- **Shell layout**: A technique for visualizing centrality
- **Force-directed layout**: A popular method for visualizing community structure, and tips for improving clarity

Beyond the hairball

Pretty much any network analysis will include a visualization. Sometimes, they're even helpful. Visualizing networks is hard. They often contain more information than can fit on a page, and highly connected networks result in many edges crossing over each other. Too often, the result is a hairball, the affectionate name given to a network visualization that has too many densely packed connections to communicate anything meaningful. Creating a clear and meaningful network visualization requires understanding the available techniques and knowing when to apply them.

Different network layouts emphasize different properties. The force-directed layouts that have been used extensively in this book are good for visually identifying community structure, but can obscure individual relationships. Other methods, such as circular and shell layouts, are better for conveying individual relationships, but are only useful for smaller networks, and can obscure community structure.

Visualizations can also be improved by leaving out unnecessary information. When an entire network is too complex to understand in its entirety, it may still be possible to focus on a subset of that network. Two approaches that are demonstrated later in this chapter reduce complexity by focusing on the neighbors of individual nodes and by discarding edges below a certain weight.

The circular layout

Perhaps the simplest network layout, the **circular layout**, places the nodes of a network evenly around a circle. The benefits of this layout include the following points:

- Highlighting local structure
- Clearly showing each individual edge

Because the circular layout places all nodes around the outside of a circle, it leaves much space unused, and is best-suited for small networks.

Similarly, the center of the circle provides an excellent space to visualize edges, as long as the network is sparse enough to prevent crowding the available space.

NetworkX provides a circular layout through the `circular_layout()` function. As with all NetworkX layouts, it creates a dictionary that maps node labels to (x, y) tuples, which can then be passed as the `pos` argument to any of the drawing functions.

Applying the default circular layout to the Zachary karate club network creates a reasonably clear visualization, as follows:

```
G_karate = nx.karate_club_graph()
nx.draw_networkx(G_karate, pos=nx.circular_layout(G_karate))
```

This simple code produces the following output:

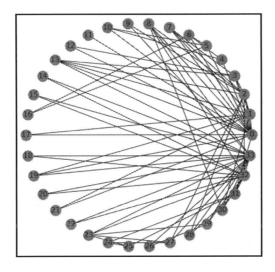

Circular layout

However, we can do even better. The default circular layout places nodes in the order they were added to the `Graph` object, which can create many unnecessary edge crossings in the visualization. While NetworkX doesn't have a built-in way to reduce those edge crossings, it is simple enough to do with a little extra work.

If groups of highly interconnected nodes are placed next to each other around the circle, then their connections will be localized, preventing unnecessary overlaps and highlighting community structure. The following code copies a `Graph` object, reordering the nodes to group them by community:

```
import networkx.algorithms.community as nxcom

def community_net(G_in):
    G_out = nx.Graph()
    node_color = []
    node_community = {}
    communities = nxcom.greedy_modularity_communities(G_in)
    for i, com in enumerate(communities):
        for v in com:
            G_out.add_node(v)
            node_color.append(get_color(i))
            node_community[v] = i
    G_out.add_edges_from(G_in.edges())
    return node_color, node_community, G_out
```

The preceding code uses `greedy_modularity_communities()` (discussed in Chapter 7, *In-Between - Communities*) to identify communities, and then copies nodes into a new `Graph`, one community at a time. This code also uses the `get_color()` function defined in Chapter 7, *In-Between - Communities*. The following code applies this function to the karate club:

```
node_color, node_community, G = community_net(G_karate)
nx.draw_networkx(G, pos=nx.circular_layout(G), node_color=node_color)
```

This code produces a slightly less cluttered visualization, with a much clearer community structure:

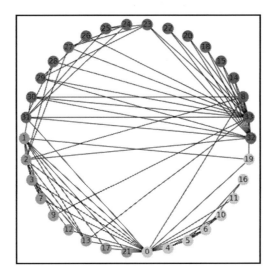

Circular layout ordered by community

The shell layout

If you liked the circle layout, you'll love the **shell layout**—it's just a lot of circles. The shell layout places nodes in concentric circles. Its benefits include the following:

- Can visualize more nodes than a circular layout in the same space
- More central nodes can be placed closer to the center to convey centrality information

However, the shell layout still does not capture community structure well, and can obscure some edges.

The following code uses the NetworkX `shell_layout()` function to visualize the karate club network. It's possible to use the default settings, but this example also uses community detection to place related nodes in similar locations:

```
degrees = dict(G.degree())
labels = sorted(degrees.keys(), key=lambda x: degrees[x], reverse=True)
nlist = []
i, k = 0, 6
while i < len(labels):
    shell_labels = labels[i:i+k]
    ordered_labels = sorted(shell_labels, key=lambda x: node_community[x])
    nlist.append(ordered_labels)
    i += k
    k += 12
pos = nx.shell_layout(G, nlist=nlist)
cm = plt.get_cmap('cool')
nx.draw_networkx(
    G, pos, alpha=1, node_color=node_color, with_labels=True)
```

Running this code produces the following visualization:

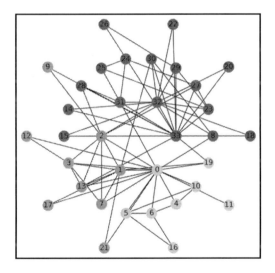

Shell layout

Note that the highest degree nodes, including John A. and Mr. Hi, are in the centermost circle, with the least connected nodes around the edge.

The force-directed layout

The **force-directed** layout is a great visualization for many networks, and is a good go-to for your first visualization of a network. It works by repeatedly pushing all nodes apart and then pulling connected nodes back toward each other. It is benefits include the following:

- Accommodates large networks
- Clearly conveys community structure

However, the force-directed layout is also one of the most hairball-prone methods, particularly if there is one large community pulling all nodes together. It works best in sparser networks with multiple communities.

In Chapter 3, *From Data to Networks*, we saw that a default force-directed layout of the *Frankenstein* word co-occurrence network wasn't particularly informative. Now, we'll return to that example to demonstrate ways to focus on different aspects of a network and reduce clutter. The code to load the network is exactly the same as in Chapter 3, *From Data to Networks*, and is omitted here. The resulting network is G_frank.

Null models

Edge weights can be adjusted to identify particularly significant edges using a null model. **Null models** are sets of assumptions that are used to predict the strength of an edge, which can be used to identify edges that surpass those predictions. This might seem familiar because the gravity model that we used in the previous chapter is an example of a null model. Here, we will use a simpler model , assuming that the weight of an edge is proportional to the product of the degrees of the endpoints. The following function takes a Graph as input and produces a new copy with a log_residual edge property representing the deviation of each edge from its predicted weight:

```
import math
def residual_net(G):
    G_residual = nx.Graph(G)
    # Calculate weighted degrees
    degrees = dict((v, 0) for v in G_residual.nodes)
    for e in G_residual.edges:
        v, w = e
        degrees[v] += G_residual.edges[e]['count']
        degrees[w] += G_residual.edges[e]['count']
    # Calculate total edge weight in network
    M = sum([G_residual.edges[e]['count'] for e in G_residual.edges])
    # Find residual weight for each node pair
    for v in G_residual.nodes:
```

```
        for w in G_residual.nodes:
            dv = degrees[v]
            dw = degrees[w]
            # Only count each edge once
            if v >= w:
                continue
    # Expected fraction of weights associated with each endpoint
            # Factor of two adjusts normalization for excuding v >= w
            expected = (dv / M / 2) * (dw / M / 2) * 2 * M
            if expected == 0:
                continue
            try:
                count = G_residual.edges[v, w]['count']
                log_residual = math.log10(count) - math.log10(expected)
                G_residual.edges[v, w]['log_residual'] = log_residual
            except KeyError:
                continue
    return G_residual

# Generate residual network
G_residual = residual_net(G_frank)
```

Now that we have the residual edge weights, we can take the additional step of discarding any edges below a certain threshold. The following code also keeps only the largest connected component:

```
# Find edges with residuals above a threshold
threshold = 3.2
edges = [
    (v, w) for v, w, d in G_residual.edges(data=True)
    if d['log_residual'] > threshold]
# Create a network with only those edges
G_threshold = G_residual.edge_subgraph(edges)
# Find largest connected component
G_giant = G_threshold.subgraph(max(nx.connected_components(G_threshold),
key=len))
```

Before visualizing, we'll take one last step. By default, the force-directed layout starts with random positions, which is less than ideal. Sometimes, closely related nodes will get stuck on opposite sides of the visualization just because of where they started. The following code detects communities and creates a circular layout based on those communities. This layout can then be used as a starting point for the force-directed layout:

```
# Find communities
G = G_giant
node_color, node_community, G = community_net(G)
pos = nx.circular_layout(G)
```

```
nx.draw_networkx(
    G, pos=pos, node_size=100, node_color=node_color,
    edge_color='#999999', with_labels=False)
```

Visualizing the circular layout shows that we've successfully identified some communities within the network:

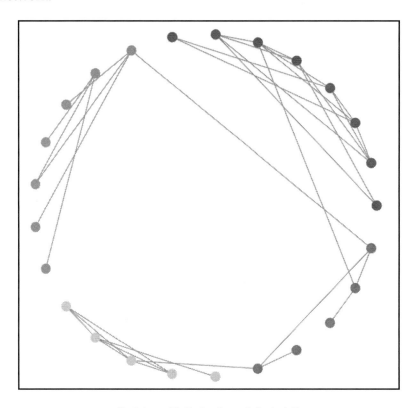

Circular layout of the *Frankenstein* network after threshold

Finally, we pass the circular layout as the `pos` parameter to `spring_layout()`:

```
plt.figure(figsize=(15,15))
pos = nx.spring_layout(G, pos=pos)
nx.draw_networkx(
    G, pos=pos, node_size=0, edge_color='#999999', with_labels=True)
# Add margin for labels
plt.xlim([-1.1, 1.1])
```

The result is a visualization that's much cleaner than the hairball we started with back in Chapter 3, *From Data to Networks*:

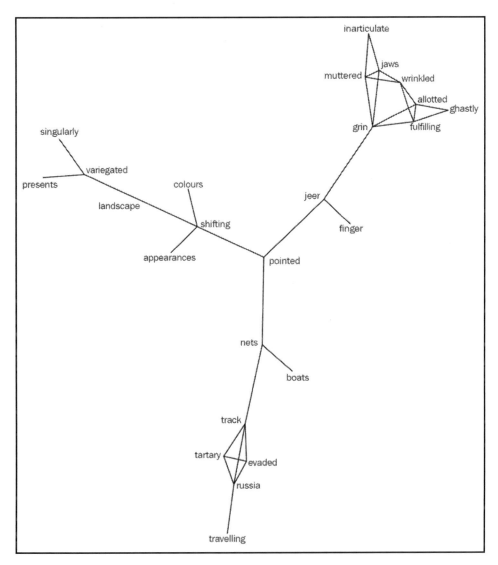

In this case, the communities correspond to different branches of the force-directed layout, which themselves correspond to particular sentences in the novel. These sentences contain words that are only used in combination with each other. The branches are unified by the word **pointed**, which is uncommon, but shared by all three.

The preceding techniques can be used to reduce the complexity of a visualization to focus on particular aspects of a network. By doing so, it's often possible to turn a hairball into a useful, if not beautiful, image.

Summary

This chapter has described several of the visualization methods provided by NetworkX, as well as ways to use them effectively. The circular layout is a clear and simple option for smaller networks. Maintaining much of the clarity of the circular layout, the shell layout can visualize more nodes in the same space and can convey centrality information. Finally, the force-directed layout can handle large networks and communicate community structure, although it is sometimes necessary to apply additional techniques to focus on particular subsets of edges. Our network adventure is now drawing to a close. The next and final chapter reviews the themes of this book, and offers some suggestions for additional resources.

12
Conclusion

By now, you should have a good understanding of the fundamentals of using NetworkX for network science. This final chapter focuses on what you can do with that understanding. I will review the themes and techniques presented throughout this book and try to place them into a greater context. Network science is a genuinely exciting field, and I hope this book has managed to convey the excitement of doing network science with NetworkX.

Topics in this chapter include the following:

- **The practice of network science**: Reviewing the topics covered throughout this book
- **Learning more**: Where to go next if you'd like to continue learning about networks
- **Advances in network science**: A sampling of some of the exciting ongoing work in network science
- **The impact of network science**: Understanding the wide range of applications of network science, and their consequences for society

The practice of network science

The techniques covered throughout this book have introduced many of the fundamental concepts in network science. `Chapter 2`, *Working with Networks in NetworkX*, focused on how those concepts can be applied using NetworkX. Many types of networks have appeared along the way:

- Weighted
- Directed
- Affiliation
- Layered

Understanding the differences between—and the uses of—these networks makes it easier to choose the right network for the right data. The examples throughout this book have demonstrated how to work with a wide range of data and networks.

Chapter 5, *The Small Scale – Nodes and Centrality*, to Chapter 7, *In-Between – Communities*, discussed network structure at the large, small, and medium scale. Tools such as centrality measures are best for understanding the role of an individual node within the context of a network, while tools such as community detection shed light on how groups of nodes relate to each other.

The remaining chapters paid special attention to certain types of data:

- Social networks
- Spatial networks
- Temporal networks
- Simulated networks

The different processes that give rise to these networks can create special properties, such as the small-world structure of social networks. Similarly, the different structures of these networks can result in different behaviors, such as whether or not a contagion spreads.

Learning more

While I have tried to be as broad as possible in introducing the fundamental concepts of network science, I have, no doubt, forgotten many things (including where I put several sets of earbuds). Furthermore, there has been an immense amount of work on each of the topics introduced here. So, if you've made it this far and want more, there is a lot more to learn.

There are many great resources for learning about network science. Some are listed as follows, including books, textbooks, and websites. For a more advanced understanding of network science, I highly recommend studying linear algebra, the type of mathematics used in the formal study of networks:

- *Watts, D. J. (2004). Six degrees: The science of a connected age. WW Norton & Company*
- *Barabasi, A. L. (2003). Linked: How everything is connected to everything else and what it means*

- *Easley, D., & Kleinberg, J. (2010). Networks, crowds, and markets (Vol. 8). Cambridge: Cambridge University Press*
- *Strang, G., Strang, G., Strang, G., & Strang, G. (2016). Introduction to Linear Algebra, Fifth Edition. Wellesley, MA: Wellesley-Cambridge Press*
- *Newman, M. (2018). Networks. Oxford university press*
- *Scott, J., & Carrington, P. J. (2011). The SAGE handbook of social network analysis. SAGE publications*
- *Healy, K. (2013). Using metadata to find Paul Revere* https://kieranhealy.org/blog/archives/2013/06/09/using-metadata-to-find-paul-revere/
- *Case, N. (2018). The Wisdom and/or Madness of Crowds* https://ncase.me/crowds/

NetworkX has excellent online documentation available at https://networkx.github.io/documentation/latest/. If you're curious, you can even use it to see the source code of each class and function. The documentation contains more detailed information than would fit in this book, as well as any features added after this book was written (you're in the future!).

In recent years, researchers have compiled many network data sets and made them available online. The following sites can be a great place to find data to test your network analysis skills:

- *Stanford Network Analysis Project* (Leskovec & Krevl, 2014): https://snap.stanford.edu/data
- *Index of Complex Networks* (Clauset et al., 2016): https://icon.colorado.edu Data
- *Koblenz Network Collection* (Kunegis, 2013): http://konect.uni-koblenz.de/about

Advances in network science

Networks and network science continue to be an exciting area of ongoing research. Here's a small sampling of some of the interesting work that's going on right now:

- **Multiple membership community detection**: When nodes can belong to several communities
- **Multiple edge types**: Working with networks with several distinct edge types
- **Collaborations and shocks**: How social networks influence collaboration, and how networks change during major events

- **Predicting virality**: Understanding how and why certain ideas and content spread
- **Connectomes**: Understanding the brain by studying networks of neurons or brain regions

The impact of network science

As the world becomes increasingly interconnected, network science is proving to be a useful tool for understanding those connections. Network science is used regularly to do the following:

- Predict and prevent the spread of contagious diseases
- Evaluate and improve the electric grid, road network, and other infrastructure networks
- Understand the economics of international trade
- Understand the spread of information on social media

The preceding applications might give the impression that network science is an important tool for improving society, and it absolutely can be. However, the powerful techniques of network science also raise important ethical questions. Network techniques can be used to infer information about individuals—such as their political party or sexual orientation—without that individuals consent. Similarly, network science can be used to strategically target information (or misinformation) in order to reach the most people. So, along with understanding the concepts and code libraries available for network science, it is critical to consider how and when to use those tools wisely.

Centrality measures and complex contagions aside, network science is fundamentally about relationships. Whether between people or proteins, network science is a tool for understanding how relationships are shaped and how the structure of those relationships shape the world. Hopefully, the information in this book will help you understand the relationships that matter to you and to shape your world for the better.

Appendix

The branch of mathematics studying networks is called graph theory. **Graph** and **network** are more or less two words for the same thing, but mathematicians can be picky about exact definitions. A graph is composed of two parts: a set of things called **vertices** and a set of **edges** representing connections between those vertices.

What is a vertex? It's a mathematical object whose sole purpose is to be connected to other vertices. In other words, it's pretty much the same thing as a node. In order to tell vertices apart, it is necessary to give them some kind of label. These labels could be anything, but let's call them v_1, v_2, and so on. It's a common convention to call a set of vertices V. Mathematically, this can be written using the following set notation, where N is the number of vertices in V:

$$V = \{v_1, v_2, ..., v_N\},$$

Connections between vertices are called edges, just as in NetworkX. For undirected graphs, an edge is a set of two vertices. Elements in a set don't have a particular order, so $\{v_1, v_2\}$ is the same as $\{v_2, v_1\}$, which makes sets good for undirected graphs. For directed graphs, order matters, so an edge is represented by an ordered pair of vertices. For example, (v_1, v_2) and (v_2, v_1) represent edges pointing in opposite directions. A set of edges is typically called E. Weighted edges can be represented in many ways, but one of the most practical is using a mathematical object called a matrix.

Adjacency matrices

A **matrix** is a way of describing pairwise relationships. A matrix looks like a grid of numbers, as in the following example:

```
┌              ┐
| 0     1  42  |
| 0.5  -3   1  |
└              ┘
```

The preceding matrix contains six entries, organized in two rows and three columns. A matrix can have any number of rows or columns, but they are always rectangular. A matrix with two rows and three columns is described as a 2 x 3 matrix. If the entire matrix is called A, then the element at row i and column j is called $A_{i,j}$. So, in the preceding example, $A_{2,1} = 0.5$.

One way to represent a graph as a matrix is to place the weight of each edge in one element of the matrix (or a zero if there is no edge). So, an edge from v_3, to v_1 with a weight of 37 would be represented by $A_{3,1} = 37$, meaning the third row has a 37 in the first column. This representation is called an **adjacency matrix**.

With a little thought, it can be shown that adjacency matrices are always square. The number of rows is the number of columns is the number of vertices. Similarly, there is nothing saying that $A_{i,j}$ has to be the same as $A_{j,i}$, so adjacency matrices can easily represent a directed graph. For an undirected graph, $A_{i,j}$ always equals $A_{j,i}$, so the matrix is symmetric across one diagonal.

As an example, consider this network from Chapter 1, *What is a Network?*:

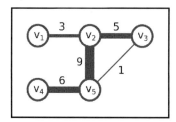

The corresponding adjacency matrix is as follows:

$$
\begin{bmatrix}
0 & 3 & 0 & 0 & 0 \\
3 & 0 & 5 & 0 & 9 \\
0 & 5 & 0 & 0 & 1 \\
0 & 0 & 0 & 0 & 6 \\
0 & 9 & 1 & 6 & 0
\end{bmatrix}
$$

Matrices are more than just grids of numbers though! There are many mathematical operations that can be used to manipulate and combine matrices. For example, addition can be defined for two matrices by adding the elements at the same row and column. These operations can correspond to meaningful network processes. One such operation is the **transpose**, which exchanges $A_{i,j}$ with $A_{j,i}$. The transpose of A is denoted as A^T and corresponds to reversing the direction of all edges.

Biadjacency matrices

Bipartite graphs can be represented using another type of matrix. Bipartite graphs have two types of vertices, which I'll call **row-vertices** and **column-vertices**, for reasons that will become obvious. All edges connect one row-vertex to one column-vertex, so it's not necessary to use a full adjacency matrix connecting all possible vertex pairs. Instead, we represent the edge from the ith row-vertex to the jth column-vertex by setting the element of the matrix at row i and column j. This type of matrix is called a **biadjacency matrix**, and is typically denoted as B. Because the number of row vertices and column vertices can be different, the biadjacency matrix does not need to be square. The bipartite graph can be projected into a graph containing only row-nodes (or only column-nodes) by using simple matrix operations.

Modularity

As an example of how math is used in network science, several popular community detection algorithms (including those discussed in Chapter 7, *In-Between – Communities*) work by maximizing a mathematical property called modularity. Modularity is the difference between the fraction of internal edges and how many you'd expect if edges were assigned randomly (without changing vertex degrees).

Let's assume an undirected network. Given a set of vertex labels c, with corresponding vertex degrees k_i for $i \epsilon c$, the expected fraction of internal edges can be approximately written as follows:

$$\Sigma_{i \epsilon c} \, \Sigma_{j \epsilon c} \, k_i k_j \, / \, (2 \, |E|)^2,$$

Here, $|E|$ is the total number of edges. The true number of edges between vertices i and j is given by element $A_{i,j}$ of the adjacency matrix. Summing over all communities c in partition C, the modularity Q, can be written in terms of the adjacency matrix as follows:

$$Q = \Sigma_{c \epsilon C} \, \Sigma_{i \epsilon c} \, \Sigma_{j \epsilon c} \, [A_{i,j} \, / \, (2 \, |E|) - k_i k_j \, / \, (2 \, |E|)^2].$$

Several community detection algorithms use matrix operations to try to maximize Q. This provides just one example of the many ways mathematical graph theory is used in network science.

Other Books You May Enjoy

If you enjoyed this book, you may be interested in these other books by Packt:

Python Machine Learning Cookbook - Second Edition
Giuseppe Ciaburro

ISBN: 9781789808452

- Use predictive modeling and apply it to real-world problems
- Explore data visualization techniques to interact with your data
- Learn how to build a recommendation engine
- Understand how to interact with text data and build models to analyze it
- Work with speech data and recognize spoken words using Hidden Markov Models
- Get well versed with reinforcement learning, automated ML, and transfer learning
- Work with image data and build systems for image recognition and biometric face recognition
- Use deep neural networks to build an optical character recognition system

Python Deep Learning - Second Edition

Ivan Vasilev

ISBN: 9781789348460

- Grasp the mathematical theory behind neural networks and deep learning processes
- Investigate and resolve computer vision challenges using convolutional networks and capsule networks
- Solve generative tasks using variational autoencoders and Generative Adversarial Networks
- Implement complex NLP tasks using recurrent networks (LSTM and GRU) and attention models
- Explore reinforcement learning and understand how agents behave in a complex environment
- Get up to date with applications of deep learning in autonomous vehicles

Leave a review - let other readers know what you think

Please share your thoughts on this book with others by leaving a review on the site that you bought it from. If you purchased the book from Amazon, please leave us an honest review on this book's Amazon page. This is vital so that other potential readers can see and use your unbiased opinion to make purchasing decisions, we can understand what our customers think about our products, and our authors can see your feedback on the title that they have worked with Packt to create. It will only take a few minutes of your time, but is valuable to other potential customers, our authors, and Packt. Thank you!

Index

Made in the USA
Columbia, SC
27 November 2021

49875326R00104